NORTHERN ONTARIO

A BIBLIOGRAPHY

NORTHERN ONTARIO

a bibliography

*compiled by
Loraine Spencer and
Susan Holland*

★ ★ ★

University of Toronto Press

© University of Toronto Press 1968

Printed in Canada
Reprinted in 2018
ISBN 978-1-4875-7318-8 (paper)

FOREWORD

The present bibliography is intended as an aid to those individuals--government personnel, researchers, students, and interested laymen--who are involved in work, both theoretical and applied, in northern Ontario, frequently referred to as the Patricias.

This volume was conceived of several years ago when, in the course of my own research and work with the Ontario government, the lack of listing of sources for northern Ontario was sorely felt. But time was not available for me to make such a compilation. Accordingly, if a work of this kind was to be assembled, assistance was needed. And assistance was fortunately forthcoming. The Royal Ontario Museum most kindly aided the preparation of the bibliography through the allocation of funds, space, and personnel, all of which are perpetually at a critical premium. To Mr. Jack Brook, Secretary-Treasurer, and Miss Eleanor Feely, Head Librarian of the Museum, who made this all possible, I shall always be grateful.

The scope of the present bibliography was to have been restricted to the area as outlined by the compilers. Here my ethnographic bias altered the situation since I requested that some items, chiefly ethnological and archaeological, from peripheral areas be included. In this I felt justified, thinking that, since so little work had been done within the area, sources on the periphery might point to the situation within.

The compilers, in so far as possible, have made a logical ordering of the sources under the appropriate categories. As can readily be imagined, some sources were difficult to place, and I am responsible for the choice of category in these instances. The entries have been cross-indexed where they warranted inclusion under more than one heading.

It was most fortunate that two highly skilled librarians were available to compile this bibliography. As an excursion into the field under special circumstances, it does not claim to be exhaustive, and the compilers welcome any suggestions or additions.

                              Edward S. Rogers
                              Curator of Ethnology
                              Royal Ontario Museum
                              Toronto

CONTENTS

Foreword	v
Introduction	ix
Archaeology	1
Botany	3
Boundary	8
Economics and Development	12
Entomology	24
Ethnology	26
Forestry	44
General	46
Geography	55
Geology and Mining	59
History	80
Ichthyology	83
Invertebrate Zoology	85
Linguistics	87
Mammalogy	90
Medicine	92
Meteorology	93
Moose Factory and Moosonee	95
Ornithology	98
Paleontology	105
Transportation	109
Author Index	115
Map of the Patricias	viii

INTRODUCTION

This bibliography lists books, periodical articles and government reports relating to the section of northern Ontario commonly called the Patricias. (See map p. viii.) The area is north of the Canadian National Railway line from Cochrane through Kapuskasing and Hearst to Sioux Lookout, north of Lake Abitibi on the east and north of Lake of the Woods on the west. The remaining boundaries are those of the province: the Ontario-Quebec border, James Bay and Hudson Bay on the east and north, and the Ontario-Manitoba border on the north and west.

Items have been arranged alphabetically by author or issuing body under broad subject headings. At the end of many sections, reference is made to entries which are relevant to the section but are cited fully elsewhere. This is done briefly, by quoting the author, short title and, in capital letters, the section heading under which the full entry will be found. In addition, users of the bibliography are referred to a general section containing items relating to several of our subject divisions. No cross references are made from this general section and no references are made to it from any of the other subject sections. In addition to subject sections, a section has been added to indicate items in all sections relating to the geographical area of Moose Factory and Moosonee.

The bibliography includes items on as wide a variety of topics as possible, but we have excluded fiction, and articles from daily newspapers and popular sports magazines. Mimeographed material, with the exception of a few theses and reports of government agencies, has also been excluded. Three periodicals have been listed in their entirety in the general section, as a full citation of their articles would have added greatly to the length of the bibliography but not greatly to its usefulness.

Entry has been made under personal author whenever possible and by issuing body when no author was indicated. In the few cases in which the government body responsible for a work has not been indicated in the imprint or series note, the name of the issuing body printed "at the head of title" has been included.

Most of the entries in the bibliography have been seen by the author responsible for the sections in which they are listed. The items preceded by an asterisk (*) in the bibliography have not been verified or not verified in their entirety. Most items were located in Toronto. The few that were not were readily available on interlibrary loan. Readers may be interested in knowing that Susan E. Holland prepared the entries in the archaeology, ethnology and linguistics sections, and Loraine M. I. Spencer is responsible for the remaining sections of the bibliography.

ARCHAEOLOGY

Dewdney, Selwyn and K. E. Kidd
    Indian rock paintings of the Great Lakes.
2d. ed. [Toronto] Published for the Quetico
Foundation by University of Toronto Press [c1967]
x, 191 p. illus.

Kenyon, W. A.
    Archaeology of the English River district.
Ontario history, v. 50, p. 52-54. 1958.

Kenyon, W. A.
    Old Fort Albany relics. Beaver, outfit 292,
p. 21-23. Summer 1961. illus.

Kenyon, W. A.
    The 'Old House' at Albany. Beaver, outfit 296,
p. 48-52. Autumn, 1965. illus.

Kenyon, W. A.
    The second season of excavation at Fort Albany.
Ontario history, v. 54, p. 128-132. 1962.

Kidd, K. E. See Dewdney, Selwyn and K. E. Kidd

Lee, T. E.
    Archaeological investigations at Lake Abitibi,
1964. Laval University. Centre d'etudes nordiques.
Travaux divers, no. 10, 1965. 58 p. illus.

Lee, T. E.
    A small beach site on the south shore of Lake
Abitibi. New world antiquity, v. 9, p. 152-161.
1962.

MacNeish, R. S.
   Archaeological investigations in the arctic and
sub-arctic. Arctic, v. 10, p. 189-190. 1957.

Ridley, Frank
   The ancient sites of Lake Abitibi. Canadian
geographical journal, v. 64, p. 86-93. 1962.
illus.

Ridley, Frank
   An archaeological reconnaissance of Lake Abitibi,
Ontario. Ontario history, v. 48, p. 18-23. 1956.
map.

Ridley, Frank
   An archaeological reconnaissance of Lake Abitibi,
Province of Ontario. Pennsylvania archaeologist,
v. 26, p. 32-35. 1956.

Ridley, Frank
   A preliminary comment on arctic regionalism.
Pennsylvania archaeologist, v. 27, p. 145-148.
1957.

Ridley, Frank
   Sites on Ghost River, Lake Abitibi. Pennsylvania
archaeologist, v. 28, p. 39-56. 1958. illus.

Skinner, Alanson
   Traces of the Stone Age among the eastern and
northern tribes. American anthropologist, v. 14,
p. 391-395. 1912.

BOTANY

Auer, Vaino
    Botany of the interglacial peat beds of Moose River basin. Canada. Geological Survey. Summary report, 1926, pt. C, p. 45-47.

Baldwin, W. K. W. and others
    Botanical excursion to the boreal forest region in northern Quebec and Ontario. Ottawa [Queen's Printer] 1959. 119 p. illus., maps.

Baldwin, W. K. W.
    Plants of the clay belt of northern Ontario and Quebec. [Ottawa] Department of Northern Affiars and National Resources, 1958. vi, 324 p. illus., maps. (Canada. National Museum. Bulletin no. 156)

Baldwin, W. K. W.
    Report on botanical excursion to the boreal forest region in northern Quebec and Ontario. Ottawa, Department of Northern Affairs and National Resources, 1962. 107 p. illus., maps.
    At head of title: National Museum of Canada.

Boivin, Bernard
    The distribution of <u>Arnica</u> <u>Wilsonii</u> Rydberg and its significance. Rhodora, v. 54, p. 200-205. 1952.

Borron, E. B.
    List of plants found near Moose in the years 1881 and 1882. <u>In</u> his Report ... on that part of the basin of Hudson's Bay belonging to the province of Ontario. Toronto, "Grip", 1884. p. 75-78.

Duman, Maximilian. <u>See</u> Dutilly, A. A., Ernest Lepage
and Maximilian Duman

Dutilly, A. A., Ernest Lepage and Maximilian Duman
    A collection of plants from Winisk, Ontario.
Naturaliste canadien, v. 86, p. 214-218. 1959.

Dutilly, A. A., Ernest Lepage and Maximilian Duman
    Contribution à la flore du versant occidental
de la baie James, Ontario. Washington, D. C.,
Catholic University of America, 1954. 144 p.
maps. (Catholic University of America. Arctic
Institute. Contribution no. 5F)

Hustich, Ilmari
    Forest-botanical notes from the Moose River area,
Ontario, Canada. Helsinki, Societas Geographica
Fenniae, 1955. 50 p. illus., maps. (Acta
geographica, v. 13, no. 2)

Kenoyer, L. A.
    Notes on plant ecology of northern Ontario.
Michigan Academy of Sciences, Arts and Letters.
Papers, v. 25, pt. 1, p. 67-74. 1940.

Kirkconnell, T. W.
    The flora of Kapuskasing. Canadian field-
naturalist, v. 33, p. 33-35. 1919.

Lepage, Ernest
    Distribution du <u>Salix pseudomonticola</u> Ball dans
le Quebec. Association canadienne-française pour
l'avancement des sciences, Montreal. Annales,
v. 15, p. 117. 1949.

Lepage, Ernest
    Etudes sur quelques plantes Américaines.
Naturaliste canadien, v. 79, p. 177-184. 1952.
illus.

Lepage, Ernest
    Etudes sur quelques plantes Américaines, II.
  Hybrides intergénériques: Agrohordeum et Agroelymus.
  Naturaliste canadien, v. 79, p. 241-266. 1952.
  illus.

Lepage, Ernest
    Etudes sur quelques plantes Américaines, III.
  Naturaliste canadien, v. 81, p. 59-68. 1954.

Lepage, Ernest
    Etudes sur quelques plantes Américaines, VIII.
  Naturaliste canadien, v. 86, p. 67-72. 1959.
  illus.

Lepage, Ernest
    Nouveautés dans la flore de la baie James.
  Naturaliste canadien, v. 81, p. 255-261. 1954.

Lepage, Ernest. See also Dutilly, A. A., Ernest
  Lepage and Maximilian Duman

Macoun, J. M.
    List of plants collected by W. J. Wilson along
  the shore of James Bay and in the valley of the
  Kapiscan River. Canada. Geological Survey.
  Summary report, 1902. p. 239-241.

Macoun, J. M.
    List of plants collected on the Rupert and
  Moose Rivers, along the shores of James' Bay, and
  on the islands in James' Bay, during the summers
  of 1885 and 1887. Canada. Geological Survey.
  Annual report, n. s., v. 3, pt. J, p. 63-74.
  1887-1888.

Mickle, G. R.
    The increase of the food supply for ducks in
  northern Ontario, with description of edible plants
  by R. B. Thomson. Toronto, King's Printer, 1913.
  17 p. illus.

Moir, D. R.
   A floristic survey of the Severn River drainage basin of northwestern Ontario. Ann Arbor, Mich., University Microfilms, 1959. iv, 261 ℓ. illus. (University of Minnesota. PhD dissertation)

Persson, Herman and H. M. Sjörs
   Some bryophytes from the Hudson Bay lowland of Ontario. Svensk botanish tidskrift, v. 54, p. 247-268. 1960. map.

Porsild, A. E.
   <u>Nymphaea tetragona</u> Georgi in Canada. Canadian field-naturalist, v. 53, p. 48-50. 1939.

Potter, David
   Plants collected in the southern region of James Bay. Rhodora, v. 36, p. 274-284. 1934. map.

Sjörs, H. M.
   Bogs and fens in the Hudson Bay lowlands. Arctic, v. 12, p. 2-19. 1959. illus., maps.

Sjörs, H. M.
   Bogs and fens on Attawapiskat River, northern Ontario. Canada. National Museum. Bulletin no. 186, p. 45-133. 1963. illus., maps.

Sjörs, H. M.
   Forest and peatland at Hawley Lake, northern Ontario. Canada. National Museum. Bulletin no. 171, p. 1-31. 1961. illus., map.

Sjörs, H. M.   <u>See also</u> Persson, Herman and H. M. Sjors

Thomson, R. B.   <u>See</u> Mickle, G. R.

Botany

SEE ALSO

Barnston, George
    Observations on the progress of the seasons as affecting animals and vegetables at Martin's Falls
        MAMMALOGY

Holmes, E. M.
    ... Medicinal plants used by the Cree Indians
        ETHNOLOGY

Hustich, Ilmari
    On the phytogeography of the subarctic Hudson Bay lowland
        GEOGRAPHY

Mickle, G. R.
    Possibilities of northern Ontario as a breeding ground for ducks
        ORNITHOLOGY

Potter, David
    Botanical evidence of a post-Pleistocene marine connection between Hudson Bay and the St. Lawrence basin
        GEOLOGY

Preble, E. A.
    A biological investigation of the Hudson Bay region
        MAMMALOGY

BOUNDARY

Canada. Ontario-Manitoba Boundary Commission, 1954
    Report of the commissioners on the survey of the boundary between the provinces of Ontario and Manitoba from the twelth base line of the system of the Dominion Lands Surveys to the southern shore of Hudson Bay and the retracement and restoration of the boundary from the northwest angle of the Lake of the Woods to the Winnipeg River. Ottawa, Queen's Printer, 1955. 92 p. illus., map.

Canada. Parliament. House of Commons. Select Committee on boundaries between Ontario and unorganized territories
    Report of the Select committee on the boundaries between the province of Ontario and the unorganized territories of the Dominion. Ottawa, Maclean, Roger, 1880. xxviii, 480 p.

Financial Post
    Ontario wins 200-acre slice as Manitoba boundary drawn. Fiancial post, v. 48, p. 8. May 1, 1954.

Great Britain. Privy Council
    In the matter of the boundary between the provinces of Ontario and Manitoba, in the Dominion of Canada. [London, Clowes, n. d.] 2 v.
    Copy examined had no title page.

Hincks, Francis
    The northerly and westerly boundaries and the province of Ontario, and the award relating thereto, on discussed and explained... in his public lecture at the Education Department, Toronto, May 6th, 1881. Toronto, C. Blackett Robinson, 1881. 32 p.

Boundary

Lindsey, Charles
    An investigation of the unsettled boundaries of
Ontario. Toronto, Hunter, Rose, 1873. 250 p.
maps.

MacMahon, Hugh
    Statement of the case of the government of the
Dominion of Canada regarding the boundaries of the
province of Ontario. London, Ont., 1878. 20 ℓ.
map.

Mills, David
    A report on the boundaries of the province of
Ontario. Toronto, Hunter, Rose, 1873. vii, 418 p.
maps.

Mills, David
    Report on the boundaries of the province of
Ontario, containing in part the substance of a
report prepared for the government of the province
in 1872, and afterwards revised and considerably
enlarged for the purposes of the arbitration between
the Dominion of Canada and the province of Ontario.
Toronto, Hunter, Rose, 1877. v, 204 p.

Natural Resources, Canada
    Fixing the Ontario-Manitoba boundary. Natural
resources, Canada, v. 10, no. 3, p. 2. March 1931.

Ontario
    Memorandum relating to the Hudson Bay territory
north of the Province of Ontario. Toronto, King's
Printer, 1905. 91 ℓ.

Ontario
    North western Ontario: its boundaries, resources
and communications. Toronto, Hunter, Rose, 1879.
iv, 64 p. map.

Ontario
    Papers presented to the House of Assembly of the

province of Ontario and resolutions moved in the
session of 1882, on the subject of the boundary
award. Toronto, C. Blackett Robinson, 1882. 56 p.
map.

Ontario
　　Statutes, documents and papers bearing on the
discussion respecting the northern and western
boundaries of the province of Ontario, including
the principal evidence supposed to be either for
or against the claims of the province. Toronto,
Hunter, Rose, 1878. ix, 448 p.

Ontario. Attorney-General's Department
　　Reports of the stipendiary magistrates with
respect to the northerly and westerly parts of the
province of Ontario. Toronto, C. Blackett Robinson,
1880. 46 p. map.

Ontario. Attorney-General's Department, appellant vs.
　Manitoba. Attorney-General's Department, respondent
　　Ontario boundaries before the Privy Council,
1884. N. p., n. d. [1352] p.

Ontario. Attorney-General's Department, appellant vs.
　Manitoba. Attorney-General's Department, respondent
　　The proceedings before the Judicial Committee of
Her Majesty's Imperial Privy Council on the special
case respecting the westerly boundary of Ontario
... 1884, with notes.... Toronto, Warwick, 1889.
421 p. map.

Ontario. Legislative Assembly
　　Correspondence, papers and documents, of dates
from 1856 to 1882 inclusive, relating to the
northerly and westerly boundaries of the province
of Ontario. Toronto, C. Blackett Robinson, 1882.
xxvii, 504 p. map.

Ontario. Provincial Secretary's Department
　　A statement of the case of the province of Ontario respecting the westerly and northerly

Boundary

    boundaries of the province (prepared for the
    arbitration between the Dominion and the province).
    Toronto, 1879. 11 p.

Peters, F. H. and L. V. Rorke
    Report of the commissioners appointed to delimit
    the boundary between the provinces of Manitoba and
    Ontario from Winnipeg River northerly. Ottawa,
    Topographical Survey of Canada, 1925. vii, 95 p.
    illus.

Ramsay, T. K.
    Report on the northern and western limits of
    Ontario. N. p. [1873] 38 p.

Report of a select committee of the Legislative
    Assembly of the Province of Kewaydin upon the
    boundaries of the adjoining province of Ontario.
    Winnipegoosis, Knisteneaux Printing Company, 1884.
    iv, 54 p. map.

Report of proceedings before the arbitrators in the
    matter of the boundaries of the province of Ontario.
    Toronto, C. Blackett Robinson, 1880. 68 p.

Rorke, L. V.   See Peters, F. H. and L. V. Rorke

SEE ALSO

Natural Resources, Canada
    Tapping a new hinterland
      ECONOMICS AND DEVELOPMENT

ECONOMICS AND DEVELOPMENT

Bell, Robert
    On the commercial importance of Hudson's Bay, with remarks on recent surveys and investigations. Proceedings of the Royal Geographical Society, n. s., v. 3, p. 577-586. 1881. map.

Boissonneau, A. N. See Ontario. Department of Lands and Forests

Chisholm, Paul
    Chart comeback for Cobalt as silver price rises. Monetary times, v. 130, p. 77. Nov. 1962.

Chisholm, Paul
    1962 year of expansion for northeastern Ontario. Monetary times, v. 130, p. 44, 46. Nov. 1962.

Chisholm, Paul
    Now import 97% of vegetables into area [northeastern Ontario] Monetary times, v. 129, p. 46, 48, 52-53. Oct. 1961.

Clarkson, S. W.
    Northeastern Ontario: no boom but a bustling economy. Monetary times, v. 131, p. 23. Nov. 1963.

Cringan, A. T. See de Vos, Anton and A. T. Cringan

Crooks, G. E.
    James Bay public library, Moose Factory. Ontario library review, v. 43, p. 23-26. Feb. 1959. illus.

Economics and Development

Curran, G. B.
   Northern land of promise; five million acres of cut-over land available for settlement in Cochrane North district - twenty years of settlement proves what can be done. Canadian countryman, v. 33, no. 20, p. 5, 36-37. Sept. 1944. illus.

de Vos, Anton and A. T. Cringan
   Fur management in Ontario. Canadian geographical journal, v. 55, p. 62-69. 1957.

Douglass, D. P.
   Hydro-electric development for the mining industry of northern Ontario. Toronto, King's Printer, 1944. 36 p. illus., map. (Ontario. Department of Mines. Bulletin no. 46, rev. ed. Jan. 1944)

Duffell, S., A. S. MacLaren and R. H. C. Holman
   Red Lake-Lansdowne House area, northwestern Ontario; bedrock geology, geophysical and geochemical investigations. [Ottawa] Department of Mines and Technical Surveys [1963] 15 p. maps. (Canada. Geological Survey. Paper 63-5)

Duffell, S.
   "Roads to resources"; western Ontario project. Canadian mining journal. v. 82, no. 4, p. 77-79. April 1961.

Enright, C. T.
   The muskeg factor in the location and construction of an Ontario Hydro service road in the Moose River basin. National Research Council, Canada.... Proceedings of the Eighth Muskeg Research Conference.... 1962. p. 42-58. illus., map.

Erentz, C.   See Mawdsey-Jones, R. H. and C. Erentz

[Field, F. W.]
   The resources and trade prospects of northern Ontario. Toronto, Board of Trade [1912] 111 p.

Financial Post
    After $11 billion production, mines yield still more riches. Financial post, v. 59, p. 71. Oct. 2, 1965.

Financial Post
    Fish, forest, game lure tourist dollar. Financial post, v. 53, p. 61-62. Sept. 12, 1959. illus.

Financial Post
    How manufacturing industries fare [northeastern Ontario] Financial post, v. 59, p. 72. Oct. 2, 1965.

Financial Post
    It's beautiful, and fishing is always good. Financial post, v. 59, p. 18. Apr. 24 suppl., 1965. illus.

Financial Post
    New chairman for northern Ontario body. [Northern economic development committee] Financial post, v. 53, p. 11. July 25, 1959.

Financial Post
    Northeast Ontario; potential "just scratched". Financial post, v. 51, p. 57. Sept. 14, 1957. map.

Financial Post
    Northwestern Ontario bursts with untapped wealth. Financial post, v. 51, p. 54. Sept. 14, 1957. map.

Financial Post
    Otter Rapids project. Financial post, v. 54, p. 54. Feb. 20, 1960. illus.

Financial Post
    Productivity of forest rises. Financial post,

v. 59, p. 71. Oct. 2, 1965. map.

Financial Post
    Propose Moosonee seaport as new industrial centre. Financial post, v. 54, p. 11. April 2, 1960.

Financial Post
    Survey problem of dredging Moosonee deepwater harbor. Financial post, v. 54, p. 63. Feb. 20, 1960. illus.

Gould, E. C.
    Government of Ontario aids area's self-help. Monetary times, v. 129, p. 56, 58-59. Oct. 1961.

Gould, E. C.
    Northeastern Ontario; its organization and outlook. Monetary times, v. 128, p. 64, 66, 70. May 1960.

Gould, E. C.
    Ontario government's role in northeastern development; a survey of regional organization. Monetary times, v. 130, p. 50, 52, 54. Nov. 1962.

Hatfield, S. S.
    Hydro builds 5-mi. earth dyke. Engineering and contract record, v. 76, no. 4, p. 64-67. April 1963. illus., map.

Henderson, Archibald
    Agricultural resources of Abitibi. Ontario. Department of Mines. Annual report, v. 14, pt. 1, p. 213-253. 1905. illus.

Henderson, Archibald
    Agricultural resources of Mattagami. Ontario. Department of Mines. Annual report, v. 15, pt. 1, p. 136-155. 1906. illus.

Hill, G. A. See Ontario. Department of Lands and Forests

Hills, G. A.
    An approach to land settlement problems in northern Ontario. Canadian journal of agricultural science, v. 23, p. 212-216. 1942.

Holman, R. H. C. See Duffell, S., A. S. MacLaren and R. H. C. Holman

Jessup, Britt
    Northeastern Ontario... rich past... booming present... glorious future. Monetary times, v. 128, p. 60-62. May 1960. illus.

Knapton, G.
    Help offered adventuresome industry [northeastern Ontario] Financial post, v. 59, p. 73. Oct. 2, 1965.

Luke, L. W.
    Can get money, but need places to use it [northeastern Ontario] Monetary times, v. 131, p. 77-78. Nov. 1963.

McAdam, Catherine
    Our chief need: men of vision. Monetary times, v. 131, p. 61-62. Nov. 1963.

Macaulay, R. W.
    "Bright, prosperous future for northeastern Ontario". Monetary times, v. 130, p. 35. Nov. 1962.

MacLaren, A. S. See Duffell, S., A. S. MacLaren and R. H. C. Holman

Marsh, W. H. C.
    For investors opportunity knocks many times and places in northeastern regions of Ontario.

Economics and Development

    Monetary times, v. 129, p. 40-42, 44. Oct. 1961. map.

Marsh, W. H. C.
    New activity in northeastern Ontario... business highlights of 1962. Monetary times, v. 130, p. 36-38, 40. Nov. 1962. map.

Marsh, W. H. C.
    North east Ontario: young men head north. Financial post, v. 52, p. 57, 60. Sept. 13, 1958.

Marsh, W. H. C.
    There's room to grow in the Northeast. Financial post, v. 53, p. 61. Sept. 12, 1959.

Mawdsey-Jones, R. H. and C. Erentz
    Moosonee now hinted door to outer space. Financial post, v. 53, p. 25, 33. June 6, 1959. illus.

Mawdsey-Jones, R. H. and C. Erentz
    We could rent rocket range to the world. Financial post, v. 53, p. 25, 33. June 6, 1959. map.

Monetary Times
    Expansion of tourism salvation of northeast. Monetary times, v. 129, p. 89-90. Oct. 1961.

Monetary Times
    Land and forest conservation and development in northeastern Ontario. Monetary times, v. 128, p. 82-84. May 1960. illus.

Monetary Times
    Monetary times northeastern Ontario regional economic survey. Monetary times, v. 129, p. 54-55. Oct. 1961.

Monetary Times
    Monetary times northeastern Ontario regional
economic survey. Monetary times, v. 130, p. 48-49.
Nov. 1962.

Monetary Times
    More than moose in the district of Cochrane.
Monetary times, v. 131, p. 72-75. Nov. 1963.
illus.

Monetary Times
    New era for hydro power for northeast zone.
Monetary times, v. 128, p. 100, 102. May 1960.

Monetary Times
    Northeastern Ontario is on the move. Monetary
times, v. 131, p. 68. Nov. 1963.

Monetary Times
    Northeastern Ontario is vast growth area.
Monetary times, v. 128, p. 52-53. May 1960. map.

Monetary Times
    Opening of Moosonee port would double population
of northeastern Ontario. Monetary times, v. 129,
p. 88. Oct. 1961.

Monetary Times
    Power opens up new northern frontier. Monetary
times, v. 131, p. 36-37. Nov. 1963.

Monetary Times
    Two thirds of Hydro's development dollar spent
in northeast. Monetary times, v. 130, p. 63. Nov.
1962. illus.

Montgomery, Paul
    Ontario's newest north; the real reasons for the
extension of the T. & N. O. railway to the shores of
James Bay. Saturday night, v. 46, p. 17, 22. July
18, 1931.

Economics and Development 19

Natural Resources, Canada
    Tapping a new hinterland; the delimitation of the Ontario-Manitoba boundary reveals great potentialities. Natural resources, Canada, v. 2, no. 4, p. 1, 3. April 1923. map.

Nickle, W. M.
    Northeastern Ontario: "a prime location for secondary industry". Monetary times, v. 129, p. 39. Oct. 1961.

Nickle, W. M.
    Northeastern Ontario... "—brightest spot on world's horizon". Monetary times, v. 128, p. 51. May 1960.

Northeastern Ontario Development Association
    Economic survey of the district of Cochrane. North Bay, 1963. iii, 186 p. maps.

Northeastern Ontario Development Association
    A report on the possible effects of a seaport at Moosonee on the economy of northeastern Ontario. North Bay [1960?] 41 ℓ. maps.

Northern Ontario, its progress under the Whitney government. N. p., n. d. 22 p.

Ontario. Commission on Kapuskasing Colony
    Report, Commission of enquiry, Kapuskasing Colony, 1920. Toronto, A. T. Wilgress, 1920. 15 p.

Ontario. Department of Commerce and Development and others
    Report of Moosonee harbour investigation; basic field surveys, 1960. Ottawa, 1961. 74, xiii ℓ.

Ontario. Department of Economics. Economic Survey Lakehead-Northwestern Ontario region. [Toronto] 1959. ix, 96 p. illus., map.

Economics and Development

Ontario. Department of Economics. Economic Survey
    The Northeastern Ontario region economic survey.
    [Toronto] 1958. ix, 82 p. illus., map.

Ontario. Department of Economics and Development.
    Applied Economics Branch
        Economic survey of the Northeastern Ontario
    region. [Toronto] 1966. vii, 222 p. illus., maps.

Ontario. Department of Lands and Forests
    A multiple land-use plan for the Glackmayer
    development area; the report of the Glackmayer
    Subcommittee of the Northern Region Land-Use
    Planning Committee. With research supplement
    by G. A. Hill and A. N. Boissonneau. [Toronto?]
    1960. x, 210 p. illus., maps.

Phillips, Alexander
    Industrial outlook brightened by new projects
    [northwestern Ontario] Financial post, v. 58,
    p. 64. Oct. 3, 1964.

Phillips, Alexander
    North west Ontario "has almost everything".
    Financial post, v. 52, p. 59. Sept. 13, 1958.

Phillips, Alexander
    Northwestern Ontario... the region. Western
    business and industry, v. 32, p. 26, 28. Nov. 1958.

Polar Record
    The use of motor tractors in northern Ontario.
    Polar record, no. 11, p. 76-81. 1936.

Roads and Engineering Construction
    Ontario hydro's Otter Rapids project booms round-
    the-clock. Roads and engineering construction,
    v. 98, no. 4, p. 100-103. April 1960. illus.

Rogers, E. S.
    A cursory examination of the fur returns from

three Indian bands of northern Ontario; 1950-1964.
[Toronto] 1966. ii, 61 p. illus., maps. (Ontario.
Department of Lands and Forests. Research Branch.
Technical Series. Research report no. 75)

Smith, R. M.
    Northern Ontario; "limits of land settlement for
the good citizen." Canadian geographical journal,
v. 23, p. 182-211. 1941. illus., maps.

Speight, T. B.
    Relative to the soil and timber in New Ontario.
N. p. [1913?] 8 p.

Treadwell, William
    The pellet makers. Canadian geographical journal, v. 72, p. 187-205. 1966. illus., maps.

Tremblay, Maurice
    North of the Great Lake lies treasure. Canadian geographical journal, v. 22, p. 287-307. 1941. illus.

Western Business and Industry
    Ontario Hydro to spend $182 million on power.
Western business and industry. v. 34, no. 5, p.
36, 38. May 1960. map.

Williamson, O. T. G.
    Northern Ontario, the workshop, an area of rich towns, many industries. Saturday night, v. 61, p. p. 4-5. Feb. 9, 1946. illus.

SEE ALSO

Adams, J. I.
    Laboratory compression tests on peat
    GEOLOGY & MINING

Bell, J. M.
    Economic resources of Moose River basin
    GEOLOGY AND MINING

Blais, J. R.
    The recurrence of spruce budworm infestations in the past century in the Lac Seul area of northwestern Ontario
    FORESTRY

Blais, J. R.
    The relationship of the spruce budworm...to the flowering condition of the balsam fir...
    FORESTRY

Blais, J. R.
    The vulnerability of balsam fir to spruce budworm attack in northwestern Ontario
    FORESTRY

Canadian Weekly Bulletin
    Along the Abitibi
    TRANSPORTATION

Clement, S. B.
    Construction of T. & N. O. Railway extension to James Bay
    TRANSPORTATION

Coombs, D. B.
    The Hudson Bay lowland
    GEOGRAPHY

Dean, W. G.
    Human geography of the lower Albany River basin
    GEOGRAPHY

Edwards, B. G.
    Developing and operating a mine on the Canadian tundra
    GEOLOGY AND MINING

Economics and Development

Gardner, Gerard
    La region de la baie James
    GEOGRAPHY

Lyon-Fellows, Evelyn
    Bridge-building on the Pagwachnan
    HISTORY

Pain, S. A.
    The way north
    HISTORY

Richards, H. G.
    James Bay
    GEOGRAPHY

Tyrrell, J. B.
    Arrivals and departures of ships
    TRANSPORTATION

ENTOMOLOGY

Bell, Robert
   List of Lepidoptera collected in the southern part of Keewatin district. Canada. Geological Survey. Annual report, n. s., v. 2, pt. G. p. 39. 1886.

Bradley, G. A.
   Feeding sites of aphids of genus _Cinara_ Curtis (Homoptera: Aphididae) in northwestern Ontario. Canadian entomologist, v. 91, p. 670-671. 1959.

Curran, C. H.
   Descriptions of new Canadian Diptera. Canadian entomologist, v. 58, p. 170-175, 211-218. 1926.

Gardiner, L. M.
   Larval description of _Acmaeops proteus_ (Kby.) (Coleopt., Ceramb.) Canadian entomologist, v. 86, p. 190-192. 1954. illus.

Jenkins, D. W. and K. L. Knight
   Ecological survey of the mosquitoes of southern James Bay. American midland naturalist, v. 47, p. 436-468. 1952. illus.

Johnson, C. W.
   Some North American Syrphidae. Psyche, v. 14, p. 75-80. June 1907.

Knight, H. H.
   Capsus simulans (Stal) and _Labops burmeisteri_ Stal recognized from the nearctic region (Hemiptera, Miridae) Canadian entomologist, v. 58, p. 59-60. 1926.

Entomology

Knight, K. L.   See Jenkins, D. W. and K. L. Knight

Notman, Howard
    Coleoptera collected at Cochrane, northern Ontario, August 22-30, 1918, with descriptions of six new species. Journal of the New York Entomological Society, v. 27, p. 92-102. 1919.

Riotte, J. C. E.
    Revision of C. J. S. Bethune's list of the butterflies of the eastern provinces of Canada as far as northern Ontario is concerned. Ontario field biologist, no. 13, p. 1-18. 1959. map.

Spieth, H. T.
    The North American Ephemeropteran species of Francis Walker. Annals of the Entomological Society of America, v. 33, p. 324-338. 1940.

Walker, E. M.
    Odonata from the Patricia portion of the Kenora district of Ontario, with description of a new species of Leucorrhinia. Canadian entomologist, v. 72, p. 4-15. 1940. illus.

ETHNOLOGY

Anderson, J. W.
   Eastern Cree Indians. Historical and Scientific Society of Manitoba. Papers, ser. 3, no. 11, p. 30-39. 1956.

Arctic Circular
   Anthropological studies among the Attawapiskat Indians. Arctic circular, v. 9, no. 1, p. 9-10. 1956.

Baldwin, W. W.
   Social problems of the Ojibwa Indians in the Collins area in northwestern Ontario. Anthropologica, v. 5, p. 51-123. 1957.

Balicki, Asen
   "Ethnic relations and marginal man in Canada": a comment. Human organization, v. 19, no. 4, p. 170-171. 1960-61.

Bell, Robert
   The "Medicine man"; or Indian and Eskimo notions of medicine. Canadian medical and surgical journal, v. 14, p. 456-462, 532-537. 1885-86.

Birket-Smith, Kaj
   Folk-wanderings and culture drifts in northern North America. Journal de la Societe des Americanistes de Paris, n. s., v. 22, p. 1-32. 1930.

Birket-Smith, Kaj
   A geographical study of the early history of the Algonquian Indians. Internationales archiv fur ethnographie, v. 24, p. 174-222. 1918.

Cameron, Duncan
    A sketch of the customs, manners, way of living
of the natives about Nipigon (1804). In Masson,
ed. Les Bourgeois de la compagnie du nord-Ouest,
v. 2. Quebec, 1890. p. [239]-300.

Canada. Dept. of Citizenship and Immigration. Indian
    affairs branch
    Indians of Ontario; an historical review.
Ottawa, 1962. 42 p.

[Canada. Dept. of Indian Affairs?]
    The James Bay treaty, treaty no. 9 (made in 1905
and 1906) and adhesions made in 1929 and 1930.
Ottawa, King's Printer, 1931. 35 p.

Canada. Dept. of Indian Affairs and Northern
    Development
    Indians of Ontario (an historical review).
Ottawa, 1966. 40 p. illus.

Chance, N. A. and John Trudeau
    Community adjustment to rapid change among the
Eskimo and Cree. North, v. 11, p. 34-39. Jan.-
Feb., 1964.

Chance, N. A. and John Trudeau
    Social organization, acculturation and inte-
gration among the Eskimo and Cree; a comparative
study. Anthropologica, v. 5, no. 1, p. 47-56.
1963.

Cooper, J. M.
    Canadian Indians live by hunting. Science
newsletter, v. 16, no. 448, p. 286-287. 1929.

Cooper, J. M.
    The Cree witiko psychosis. Primitive man,
v. 6, no. 1, p. 20-24. 1933.

Cooper, J. M.
    The culture of the northeastern Indian hunters:

a reconstructive interpretation. In Johnson, F.,
ed. Man in Northeastern North America. (Papers
of the Robert S. Peabody foundation for archaeology,
v. 3, 1946.) p. 272-305

Cooper, J. M.
    Field notes on northern Algonkian magic. Proceedings of the 23rd International Congress of
Americanists, p. 513-518. 1928.

Cooper, J. M.
    Field notes on the Ojibwa of northern Ontario.
Journal of the Washington Academy of Science, v. 19,
p. 128. 1929.

[Cooper, J. M.]
    Hysteria prevails among the Crees. El Palacio,
v. 36, p. 75-76. 1934.

Cooper, J. M.
    Is the Algonquian family hunting ground system
Pre-Columbian? American anthropologist, v. 41,
p. 66-90. 1939.

Cooper, J. M.
    Land tenure among the Indians of eastern and
northern North America. Pennsylvania archaeologist,
v. 8, no. 3, p. 55-59. 1938.

* Cooper, J. M.
    Northern Algonkian scrying and scapulimancy.
In Festschrift for P. W. Schmidt. Vienna, 1928.
p. 205-217.

Cooper, J. M.
    The northern Algonquian Supreme Being. Catholic
University of America. Anthropological series no.
2, 1934. 78 p.

Cooper, J. M.
    Primitive Indians in Canada. El Palacio, v. 26,
p. 241-246. 1929.

Cooper, J. M.
    Scapulimancy. In Essays in anthropology presented to A. L. Kroeber. Berkeley, University of California Press, 1936. p. 29-43.

Cooper, J. M.
    The shaking tent rite among Plains and forest Algonquians. Primitive man, v. 17, no. 3 & 4, p. 60-84. 1944.

Cooper, J. M.
    Snares, deadfalls and other traps of the northern Algonquians and northern Athapaskans. Catholic University of America. Anthropological series, no. 5, 1938. illus.

Dunning, R. W.
    Differentiation of status in subsistence level societies. Royal Society of Canada. Transactions, ser. III, v. 54, sect. II, p. 25-32. 1960.

Dunning. R. W.
    Ethnic relations and marginal man in Canada. Human organization, v. 18, no. 3, p. 117-122. 1959.

Dunning, R. W.
    Rules of residence and ecology among the northern Ojibwa. American anthropologist, v. 61, p. 806-816. 1959.

Dunning, R. W.
    Social and economic change among the northern Ojibwa. [Toronto] University of Toronto Press [1959] 217 p. illus.

Dunning, R. W.
    Some implications of economic change in northern Ojibwa social structure. Canadian journal of economics and political science, v. 24, p. 562-566. 1958.

Eastman, C. A.
    Life and handicrafts of the northern Ojibwas.
    Southern workman, v. 40, p. 273-278. 1911.

Ellis, C. D.
    The missionary and the Indian in central and
    eastern Canada. Arctic anthropology, v. 2, no. 2,
    p. 25-31. 1964.

Fisher, M. W.
    The mythology of the northern and northeastern
    Algonkian in reference to Algonkian mythology as
    a whole. In Johnson, F. ed. Man in northeastern
    North America. (Papers of the Robert S. Peabody
    foundation for archaeology, no. 3, 1946), p. 226-
    262.

Flannery, Regina
    Cross cousin marriage among the Cree and
    Montagnais of James Bay. Primitive man, v. 11,
    no. 1-2, p. 29-33. 1938.

Flannery, Regina
    The culture of the northeastern Indian hunters:
    a descriptive study. In Johnson, F., ed. Man in
    northeastern North America. (Papers of the Robert
    S. Peabody foundation for archaeology, v. 3, 1946)
    p. 263-271.

Flannery, Regina
    Gossip as a clue to attitudes. Primitive man,
    v. 7, no. 1, p. 8-12. 1934.

Flannery, Regina
    The position of woman among the Eastern Cree.
    Primitive man, v. 8, no. 4, p. 81-86. 1935.

Flannery, Regina
    Some aspects of Jmaes Bay recreative culture.
    Primitive man, v. 9, no. 4, p. 49-56. 1937.

Foerster, J. W.
    An Indian summer. Canadian geographical journal, v. 68, p. 156-163. 1964. illus.

[Forster, J. R.]
    A letter from Mr. John Reinhold Forster, F.R.S., to William Watson, M.D. giving some account of the roots used by the Indians in the neighbourhood of Hudson's Bay to dye porcupine quills. Royal Society of London. Philosophical transactions, v. 62, p. 54-59. 1772.

Gates, R. R.
    Pedigree study of Amerindian crosses in Canada. Journal of the Royal anthropological institute, v. 58, p. 511-532. 1928.

Gibbon, M. E.
    Trapper's wife. Beaver, outfit 292, p. 38-42. Spring 1962. illus.

Godsell, P. H.
    The Ojibwa Indian. Canadian geographical journal, v. 4, p. 50-66. 1932. illus.

Godsell, P. H.
    The Ojibwa Indian. Thunder Bay Historical Society. Annual report, v. 10, p. 21-29. 1920 [i.e. for 1919]

Godsell, P. H.
    Red hunters of the snows; an account of thirty years experience with the primitive Indian and Eskimo tribes of the Canadian north-west...London, Robert Hale Ltd., 1938. 324 p. illus., map.

Godsell, P. H.
    "Relief" in the sub-Arctic. Natural history, v. 38, no. 4, p. 289-291, 358. 1936.

Grant, Peter
    The Sauteux Indians (c 1804). In Masson, ed.
Les Bourgeois de la Compagnie du Nord-Ouest.
Quebec, 1890. v. 2, p. 303-366.

Hallowell, A. I.
    Aggression in Saulteaux society. Psychiatry,
v. 3, no. 3, p. 395-407, 1940.

Hallowell, A. I.
    Cross-cousin marriage in the Lake Winnipeg
area. Philadelphia Anthropological Society.
Publications, v. 1, p. 95-110. 1937.

Hallowell, A. I.
    Cultural factors in the structuralization of
perception. In Rohrer, J. H. and M. Sherif, eds.
Social psychology at the cross-roads. New York,
1951. p. 164-195.

Hallowell, A. I.
    Culture and experience. Philadelphia, University of Pennsylvania Press. 1955. xvi, 434 p.
map. (Publications of the Philadelphia Anthropological Society, v. 4)

Hallowell, A. I.
    Culture and mental disorder. Journal of abnormal
and social psychology, v. 29, p. 1-9. 1934.

Hallowell, A. I.
    Fear and anxiety as cultural and individual
variables in a primitive society. Journal of
social psychology, v. 9, p. 25-47. 1938.

Hallowell, A. I.
    Freudian symbolism in the dream of a Saulteaux
Indian. Man, v. 38, p. 47-48. 1938.

Hallowell, A. I.
    The incidence, character and decline of polygyny

among the Lake Winnipeg Cree and Saulteaux.
American anthropologist, v. 40, p. 235-256. 1938.

Hallowell, A. I.
Kinship terms and cross cousin marriage of the
Montagnais-Naskapi and the Cree. American anthropologist, v. 34, no. 2, p. 171-199. 1932.

* Hallowell, A. I.
Magic: the role of conjuring in Saulteaux
society. In May, M. A., ed. Papers presented
before the Monday Night group, 1939-1940. New
Haven, 1940. p. 94-115.

Hallowell, A. I.
Myth, culture and personality. American anthropologist, v. 49, p. 544-556. 1947.

Hallowell, A. I.
Notes on the material culture of the Island
Lake Saulteaux. Journal de la Société des
Américanistes de Paris, n. s., v. 30, p. 129-140.
1938.

Hallowell, A. I.
Ojibwa ontology, behaviour and world view.
In Diamond, S., ed. Culture in history: essays
in honor of Paul Radin. New York, Columbia
University Press, 1960. p. 19-52.

Hallowell, A. I.
Ojibwa personality and acculturation. Proceedings of the 29th International Congress of
Americanists, pt. 2, p. 105-112. 1949.

Hallowell, A. I.
Pagan tribe in Ontario. El Palacio, v. 33,
p. 204-205. 1932.

Hallowell, A. I.
The passing of the Midewiwin in the Lake Winnipeg

region. American anthropologist, v. 38, no. 1, p. 32-51. 1936.

Hallowell, A. I.
    Psychic stresses and culture patterns. American journal of psychiatry, v. 92, p. 1291-1310. 1936.

Hallowell, A. I.
    Psychosexual adjustment, personality and the Good Life in a non-literate society. In Psychosexual development in health and disease. Proceedings of the 38th meeting of the American Psychopathological Association. New York, Greene & Stratton, 1949. p. 102-123.

Hallowell, A. I.
    The role of conjuring in Saulteaux society. Philadelphia, University of Pennsylvania Press, 1942. 96 p. illus. (Publications of the Philadelphia Anthropological Society, v. 2)

Hallowell, A. I.
    Shabwan: a dissocial Indian girl. American journal of orthopsychiatry, v. 8, p. 329-340. 1938.

Hallowell, A. I.
    Sin, sex and sickness in Saulteaux belief. British journal of medical psychology, v. 18, no. 2, p. 191-197. 1939.

Hallowell, A. I.
    The size of Algonkian hunting territories: a function of ecological adjustment. American anthropologist, v. 51, no. 1, p. 35-45. 1949.

Hallowell, A. I.
    The social function of anxiety in a primitive society. American sociological review, v. 6, p. 869-881. 1941.

Hallowell, A. I.
    Some empirical aspects of northern Saulteaux

religion. American anthropologist, v. 36, no. 3, p. 389-404. 1934.

Hallowell, A. I.
    Some European folktales of the Berens River Saulteaux. Journal of American folklore, v. 52, p. 155-179. 1939.

Hallowell, A. I.
    Some psychological aspects of measurement among the Saulteaux. American anthropologist, v. 44, p. 62-77. 1942.

Hallowell, A. I.
    Some psychological characteristics of the northeastern Indians. In Johnson, F., ed. Man in Northeastern North America. (Papers of the Robert S. Peabody foundation for archaeology, v. 3, 1946) p. 195-225.

Hallowell, A. I.
    The spirits of the dead in Saulteaux life and thought. Journal of the Royal anthropological institute, v. 70, no. 1, p. 29-51. 1940.

Hallowell, A. I.
    Temporal orientation in western civilization and in a primitive society. American anthropologist, v. 39, p. 647-670. 1937.

Hallowell, A. I.
    Values, acculturation and mental health. American journal of orthopsychiatry, v. 20, p. 732-743. 1950.

Hallowell, A. I.
    Was cross-cousin marriage practised by the north-central Algonkian? Proceedings of the 23rd International Congress of Americanists, p. 519-544. 1928.

Hoffmann, Hans
    Assessment of cultural homogeneity among the James Bay Cree. New Haven, Yale University Press, 1957. iv, 301 p.

Hoffmann, Hans
    Culture change and personality modification among the James Bay Cree. Alaska University. Anthropological papers, v. 9, no. 2, p. 81-91. 1961.

Holmes, E. M.
    Notes on recent donations to the Museum of the Pharmaceutical Society. IV. Medicinal plant used by the Cree Indians, Hudson's Bay territory. Pharmaceutical journal and transactions, ser. 3, v. 15, p. 302-304. 1884.

Honigmann, J. J.
    Attawapiskat - blend of traditions. Anthropologica, v. 6, p. 59-67. 1958.

Honigmann, J. J.
    The Attawapiskat Swampy Cree; an ethnographic reconstruction. Alaska. University. Anthropological papers, v. 5, no. 1, p. 23-82. 1956.

Honigmann, J. J.
    Circumpolar forest North America as a modern culture area. In Wallace, A.F.C., ed. Men and cultures. Philadelphia, 1960. p. 447-451. (Selected papers of the 5th International Congress of Anthropological and Ethnological Sciences, Philadelphia, 1956)

Honigmann, J. J.
    Culture patterns and human stress. Psychiatry, v. 13, no. 1, p. 25-34. 1950.

Honigmann, J. J.
    Foodways in a muskeg community: an anthropo-

logical report on the Attawapiskat Indians. Canada. Dept. of Northern Affairs and national resources. Northern co-ordination & research centre, 1961. ix, 216 p. map.

Honigmann, J. J.
Incentives to work in a Canadian Indian community. Human organization, v. 8, no. 4, p. 23-28. 1949.

Honigmann, J. J.
Interpersonal relations and ideology in a northern Canadian community. Social forces, v. 35, no. 4, p. 365-370. 1957.

Honigmann, J. J.
The logic of the James Bay survey. Dalhousie review, v. 30, p. 377-386. 1951.

* Honigmann, J. J.
People of the muskeg: a multi-valence ethnographic study. Research preview (Institute for research in social science, University of N. Carolina) v. 4, no. 4, p. 11-19. 1956.

Honigmann, J. J.
Social organization of the Attawapiskat Cree Indians. Anthropos, v. 48, no. 5-6. p. 809-816. 1953.

Howard, S. H.
New day on James Bay dawning for Indians. Saturday night, v. 63, p. 12-13. Apr. 17, 1948.

Jenkins, W. H.
Notes on the hunting economy of the Abitibi Indians. Catholic University of America. Anthropological series no. 9, 1939. 31 p. illus.

Jenness, Diamond
The Indians of Canada. Canada. National Museum.

Bulletin no. 65, 1932. x, 446 p. illus., maps.

Johnson, Frederick, ed.
    Man in northeastern North America. Andover, Mass., Phillips Academy, 1946. xi, 347 p. illus., maps. (Papers of the Robert S. Peabody foundation for archaeology, v. 3)

Laviolette, Gontran
    Notes on the aborigines of the Province of Ontario. Anthropologica, v. 4, p. 79-106. 1957. maps.

Leechman, Douglas
    The savages of James Bay. Beaver, outfit 276, p. 14-17. June, 1945.

Leechman, Douglas
    Wigwam and teepee. Beaver, outfit 275, p. 28-31. December, 1944. illus.

Leechman, Douglas. See Scott, Lloyd and Douglas Leechman

Liebow, Elliott and John Trudeau
    A preliminary study of acculturation among the Cree Indians of Winisk, Ontario. Arctic, v. 15, no. 3, p. 190-204. 1962. maps.

Long Lance, Buffalo Child
    When the Crees moved west. Ontario. Annual archaeological reports, 34th, p. 25-34. 1923.

Macfie, John
    Crafts of the Cree. Beaver, outfit 288, p. 53-57. Autumn, 1957. illus.

Macfie, John
    Ojibwa craftsmen. Beaver, outfit 290, p. 34-37. Winter, 1959. illus.

Ethnology

* Michelson, Truman
    Ethnological researches in Maine, Canada and
Labrador. Smithsonian miscellaneous collections,
v. 71, no. 10, p. 99-104. 1924.

Morris, Alexander
    The treaties of Canada with the Indians of
Manitoba and the Northwest Territories, including
the negotiations on which they were based, and
other information relating thereto. Toronto,
Belfords, Clarke & Co., 1880. 375 p.

Morris, J. L.
    Indians of Ontario. Toronto, Ontario Dept. of
Lands and Forests, 1943. 75 p. map.

* Morris, W. J.
    Report to the Department of Citizenship and
Immigration concerning the integration of Indians
in the district of Red Lake, Ontario. Toronto,
University of Toronto, Dept. of Anthropology, 1958.

Ness, M. E.
    Free lives not free. Saturday night, v. 66,
p. 11. Jan. 2, 1951. illus.

Omand, D. M.
    A tour of the Patricias; a photo story. Sylva,
v. 17, p. 37-41. January-February 1961.

Ontario Housing
    Red Lake: an experiment in housing for Indians.
Ontario housing, v. 10, p. 11-15. Feb., 1964.
illus.

Orchard, W. C.
    Old porcupine-quill work. New York. Museum
of the American Indian (Heye Foundation) Indian
notes, v. 1, no. 3, p. 137-161. 1924. illus.

[Orr, R. B.]
    The Crees of New Ontario. Ontario. Annual archaeological reports, 34th, p. 9-24. 1923. map.

[Orr, R. B.?]
    New Ontario. The Algonquins. Ontario. Annual archaeological reports, 24th, p. 7-15. 1912. illus.

Rae, John
    On the condition and characteristics of some of the native tribes of the Hudson's Bay Company's territories. Royal Society of Arts. Journal, v. 30, no. 1531, p. 483-496. 1882.

Riddiough, Norman
    Treaty time at Lac Seul. Beaver, outfit 29, p. 10-13. Summer, 1962. illus.

Rogers, E. S.
    Changing settlement patterns of the Cree-Ojibwa of northern Ontario. Southwestern journal of anthropology, v. 19, no. 1, p. 64-88. 1963.

Rogers, E. S.
    The fur trade, the government and the central Canadian Indian. Arctic anthropology, v. 2, no. 2, p. 37-40. 1964.

Rogers, E. S.
    Leadership among the Indians of eastern subarctic Canada. Anthropologica, n. s., v. 7, no. 2, p. 263-284. 1965.

Rogers, E. S.
    The Round Lake Ojibwa. Toronto. Royal Ontario Museum. Art and archaeology division. Occasional paper no. 5, 1962. 280 p. illus., maps.

Rogers, E. S.
    The spirits still speak in the forest...Varsity

Rogers, E. S.
    Subsistence areas of the Cree-Ojibwa of the
    eastern sub-arctic; a preliminary study. Canada.
    National museum. Bulletin no. 204, p. 59-90. 1967.

Saindon, J. E.
    Mental disorders among the James Bay Cree.
    Primitive man, v. 6, no. 1, p. 1-12. 1933.

Scott, Lloyd and Douglas Leechman
    The Swampy Cree. Beaver, outfit 283, p. 26-27.
    Dec., 1952. illus.

Skinner, Alanson
    Bear customs of the Cree and other Algonkian
    Indians of northern Ontario. Ontario history, v.
    12, p. 203-209. 1914.

Skinner, Alanson
    The Cree Indians of northern Canada. Southern
    workman, v. 38, p. 78-83. 1909.

Skinner, Alanson
    Notes on the eastern Cree and northern Sault-
    eaux. American Museum of Natural History.
    Anthropological papers, no. 9, 1911. 116 p.

Skinner, Alanson
    Some remarks on the culture of eastern near-
    Arctic Indians. Science, v. 29, p. 150-152. 1909.

* Skinner, Alanson
    Tribes of the north. Garden City, N.J., Fron-
    tier, 1925.

Skinner, Alanson
    A visit to the Ojibway and Cree of central
    Canada. American Museum journal, v. 10, p. 9-18.
    1910. illus.

Stewart, James
    Rupert's Land Indians in the olden time. Ontario. Annual archaeological reports, 17th, p. 89-100. 1904.

* Strath, R.
    Materia medica, pharmacy and therapeutica of the Cree Indians of the Hudson Bay territory. St. Paul medical journal, v. 5, p. 735-746. 1903.

Swindlehurst, F.
    Folk-lore of the Cree Indians. Journal of American folklore, v. 18, p. 139-143. 1905.

Taylor, S. A.
    Indian, today and yesterday. Beaver, outfit 283, p. 28-31. December, 1952. illus.

Teicher, M. I.
    Windigo psychosis: a study of a relationship between belief and behaviour among the Indians of northeastern Canada. Seattle, American Ethnological Society, 1960. 129 p. map.

* Trudeau, John
    Culture change among the Cree Indians of Winish, Ontario, Canada. PhD diss., Catholic University of America, 1965.

Trudeau, John. See also Chance, N. A. and John Trudeau

Trudeau, John. See also Liebow, Elliot and John Trudeau.

Warren, W. W.
    History of the Ojibways, based upon traditions and oral statements. Collections of the Minnesota historical society, v. 5, p. 21-394. 1885.

Ethnology

SEE ALSO

Arctic Circular
    Tuberculosis Survey
    MEDICINE

East, Ben
    Waveys over the Bay
    ORNITHOLOGY

Hanson, H. C. and Andrew Gagnon
    The hunting and utilization of wild geese by the Indians of the Hudson Bay lowlands of northern Ontario
    ORNITHOLOGY

Manning, T. H.
    Exploration of James and Hudson Bays
    GEOGRAPHY

Rogers, E. S.
    A cursory examination of fur returns from three Indian bands of northern Ontario
    ECONOMICS AND DEVELOPMENT

Romig, J. H.
    James Bay geese
    ORNITHOLOGY

Tisdall, F. F. and E. C. Robertson
    Voyage of the medicine men
    MEDICINE

Vivian, R. P. and others
    The nutrition and health of the James Bay Indian
    MEDICINE

FORESTRY

Bedell, G. H. D. See MacLean, D. W. and G. H. D. Bedell

Blais, J. R.
  The recurrence of spruce budworm infestations in the past century in the Lac Seul area of northwestern Ontario. Ecology, v. 35, p. 62-71. 1954. illus., maps.

Blais, J. R.
  The relationship of the spruce budworm (Choristoneura fumiferana, Clem.) to the flowering condition of balsam fir (Abies balsamea (L) Mill.) Canadian journal of zoology, v. 30, p. 1-29. 1952. illus., map.

Blais, J. R.
  The vulnerability of balsam fir to spruce budworm attack in northwestern Ontario, with special reference to the physiological age of the tree. Forestry chronicle, v. 34, p. 405-422. 1958.

Blais, J. R. See also McGugan, B. M. and J. R. Blais

Haddow, W. R.
  Distribution and occurrence of white pine (Pinus Strobus L.) and red pine (Pinus Resinosa Ait.) at the northern limit of their range in Ontario. Journal of the Arnold Arboretum, v. 29, p. 217-226. 1948. maps.

Johnston, R. N. See Ontario. Department of Lands and Forests. Forestry Branch.

MacLean, D. W. and G. H. D. Bedell
    Northern clay belt growth and yield survey
[Ottawa, 1955] 31 p. map. (Canada. Department
of Northern Affairs and National Resourses.
Forestry Branch. Forest Research Division.
Technical note no. 20)

McGugan, B. M. and J. R. Blais
    Spruce budworm parasite studies in northwestern
Ontario. Canadian entomologist, v. 91, p. 758-783.
illus., map.

Millar, J. B.
    The silvicultural characteristics of black
spruce in the clay belt of northern Ontario.
[Toronto] 1936. 81 ℓ. (University of Toronto.
M.S.F. thesis)

Ontario. Department of Lands and Forests. Forestry
    Branch
    Report of James Bay forest survey; Moose River
lower basin, under supervision R. N. Johnston and
J. F. Sharpe, 1922. Toronto, King's Printer, 1923.
16 p. map.

Sharpe, J. F. See Ontario. Department of Lands and
    Forests. Forestry Branch

SEE ALSO

Lepage, Ernest
    Distribution du Salix pseudomonticola Ball dans
  le Quebec
    BOTANY

GENERAL

Adams, H. P. See Curran, W. T. and H. P. Adams

Anderson, David
    The net in the Bay; or, Journal of a visit to Moose and Albany. London, T. Hatchard, 1854. xvi, 276 p. map.

Anderson, J. W.
    Fur trader's story. Toronto, Ryerson [1961] xv, 245 p.

Anderson, J. W.
    Mission to Musko; stories and photos. Beaver, outfit 276, p. 3-6. March 1946. illus.

Baker, M. B.
    Lake Abitibi area. Ontario. Department of Mines. Annual report, v. 18, pt. 1, p. 263-283. 1909. illus.

Barnell, J. D.
    Christmas at Moose Factory; photographs. Beaver, outfit 281, p. 19-22. Dec. 1950.

Batty, Beatrice (Stebbing)
    Forty-two years amongst the Indians and Eskimo; pictures from the life of the Right Reverend John Horden, first Bishop of Moosonee. London, Religious Tract Society, 1893. 223 p. illus., map.

* Beaulieu, Vincent
    Aux sources de l'Albany. Messager Canadian du Sacré Coeur, v. 33, p. 517-521, 559-563. 1924.

General   47

Bell, Robert
    Report on an exploration in 1865 [i.e. 1875]
between James Bay and Lakes Superior and Huron.
Canada. Geological Survey. Report of progress,
1875-76, p. 294-342.

Bell, Robert
    Report on an exploration of portions of the
At-ta-wa-pish-kat & Albany Rivers, Lonely Lake to
James' Bay. Montreal, Dawson, 1887. 38 p. illus.
(Canada. Geological Survey. Annual report, n. s.,
v. 2, pt. G. 1886)

Bell, Robert
    Report on an exploration of the east coast of
Hudson's Bay, 1877. Montreal, Dawson, 1879. 37 p.
illus. (Canada. Geological Survey. Report of
progress, 1877-1878, pt. C)

Bell, Robert
    Report on Hudson's Bay and some of the lakes and
rivers lying to the west of it. Montreal, Dawson,
1881. 113 p. illus. (Canada. Geological Survey.
Report of progress, 1879-1880, sect. C)

Bentley, J. M.
    A canoe trip to Hudson Bay. Rod and gun and
motor sports in Canada, v. 9, p. 607-620. 1907.
illus.

[Blue, Archibald]
    The new Ontario. Ontario. Department of Mines.
Annual report, v. 5, p. 191-211. 1895.

Bolton, L. L.
    Round Lake to Abitibi River. Ontario. Department of Mines. Annual report, v. 12, p. 173-190.
1903.

Borron, E. B.
    Report... on that part of the basin of Hudson's
Bay belonging to the province of Ontario. Toronto,

"Grip", 1884. 78 p.

Borron, E. B.
    Report on the basin of Moose River and adjacent country belonging to the province of Ontario. Toronto, Warwick, 1890. ix, 94 p. maps.

Bruemmer, Fred
    Moosonee and Moose Factory. Canadian geographical journal, v. 55, p. 24-29. 1957. illus., map.

Buckman, Eduard
    Christmas at Moose Factory. Beaver, outfit 273, p. 32-35. Dec. 1942. illus.

Burwash, E. M.
    A geological reconnaissance into Patricia. Ontario. Department of Mines. Annual report, v. 29, pt. 1, p. 157-192. 1920. illus., maps.

Camsell, Charles
    Country around the headwaters of the Severn River. Canada. Geological Survey. Summary report, 1904, p. 143-152.

Caron, Ivanhoe. *See* Troyes, Pierre

Charlton, J. L.
    English River hermit; story and pictures. Beaver, outfit 276, p. 28-29. Sept. 1945. illus.

Charlton, W. A.
    Hudson's Bay railway route via Missanabie and valley of Moose River. Toronto, Warwick & Butler, 1898. 22 p. illus., maps.

Cole, A. A.
    Ontario's route to the sea. Canadian geographical journal, v. 5, p. 130-153. 1932. illus., maps.

Cotter, J. L. and Clifford Wilson
    Moose Factory; today and yesterday; photographs.

General 49

    Beaver, outfit 277, p. 22-29.　June 1946.

Curran, W. T. and H. P. Adams
    Glimpses of north-eastern Canada; a land of hidden treasure.　[Ottawa, King's Printer, 1912?]　44 p.　illus., map.
    At head of title: Canada. Department of the Interior.　Railway Lands Branch

Dowling, D. B.
    The west side of James Bay.　Canada. Geological Survey.　Summary report, 1901, p. 107-115.　map.

Fernow, B. E.
    Conditions in the clay belt of New Ontario. Ottawa, Commission of Conservation, 1913.　36 p. map.

Fraser, C. G.
    The teachers' trip to northern Ontario; the story of a happy week.　N. p.　[1920]　16 p.　illus.

[Gibson, T. W.]
    The hinterland of Ontario.　Ontario. Department of Mines. Annual report, v. 4, p. 101-138.　1894.

Green, J. A.
    Ogoki River holiday.　Beaver, outfit 277, p. 22-27.　March 1947.　illus.

Harrington, Lyn
    Canoe country.　Canadian geographical journal, v. 33, p. 72-88.　1946.　illus., map.

Harrington, Richard
    By paddle and portage; scenes from the English River country [photographs]　Beaver, outfit 279, p. 8-15.　March 1949.

Harrington, Richard
    Grassy Narrows; photographs.　Beaver, outfit 280,

p. 26-28. June 1949.

Harrington, Richard
　　Winter on James's Bay; photographs. Beaver, outfit 280, p. 10-15. Dec. 1949.

Harvey, Paul
　　North and north and north. Flying, v.62, no. 2. p. 22-23, 68,70, 72. February 1958. illus.

Jamieson, N. M.
　　Teachers' trip to northern Ontario, 1922. N. p., n. d. 24 p. illus.

Johnson, A. M.
　　James Bay artist, William Richards. Beaver, outfit 298, no. 1, p. 4-10. Summer 1967. illus.

Johnson, J. T. H.　See Randall, Peter and J. T. H. Johnson

Kane, H. B.
　　Harricanaw goose-runners; photos and story. Beaver, outfit 280, p. 16-19. Sept. 1949.

Kerr, H. L.
　　Exploration in Mattagani Valley. Ontario. Department of Mines. Annual report, v. 15, pt. 1, p. 116-135. 1906. illus.

Leitch, Adelaide
　　Road to Moosonee; a photo story. Forest and outdoors, v. 52, no. 10, p. 16-17. October 1956. map.

Lower, A. R. M.
　　By river to Albany. Beaver, outfit 275, p. 16-19. June 1944. illus., map.

Macfie, John
　　Retreat of the sea. Beaver, outfit 286, p. 38-43. Spring 1956. illus.

General 51

McInnes, William
    Region on the north-west side of Lake Nipigon.
Canada. Geological Survey. Summary report, 1902,
p. 206-211.

McInnes, William
    Report on a part of the North West Territories
of Canada drained by the Winisk and upper Attawa-
pishkat Rivers. Ottawa, Government Printing Bureau,
1909. 58 p. illus. (Canada. Geological Survey.
Report no. 1080)

McInnes, William
    The Winisk River, Keewatin district. Canada.
Geological Survey. Summary report, 1903, p. 100-
108.

Mackay, Hugh
    Moose Factory. Geographical magazine, v. 21,
p. 273-280. 1938. illus., map.

Miller, W. G.
    Lake Temiscaming to the height of land. Ontario.
Department of Mines. Annual report, v. 11, p. 214-
230. 1902.

Miller, W. G., comp.
    Reports on the district of Patricia recently
added to the province of Ontario. Toronto, King's
Printer, 1912. iv, 216 p. illus., maps. (Ontario.
Department of Mines. Annual report, v. 21, pt. 2.
1912)

Mills, Edwin
    Ogoki for trout. Beaver, outfit 276, p. 28-31.
March 1946. illus.

* Nevins, J. B.
    A narrative of two voyages to Hudson's Bay with
traditions of the North American Indians. London,
Society for Promoting Christian Knowledge, 1847.
iv, 156 p. illus.

Newnham, J. A.   See Shearwood, M. H.

Nipissing & James Bay Railway
    A description of the country traversed by this railway between Lake Nipissing & James Bay; giving the resources of the same, as well as the districts adjacent thereto, together with other useful information relating to Hudson's Bay and Strait. Toronto, Copp, Clark, 1884. 53 p.

Ontario Mining Association
    The miner at home, a story of northern Ontario. Toronto, 1948. 30 p. illus.

O'Sullivan, Owen
    A survey of the coast of Hudson Bay from York Factory to Severn River. Canada. Geological Survey. Summary report, 1905, p. 73-76.

O'Sullivan, Owen
    Survey of the south and west coast of James Bay. Canada. Geological Survey, Annual report, n. s., v. 16, sect. A, p. 173-179. 1904.

O'Sullivan, Owen
    Survey of the south coast of Hudson Bay from the Severn River to Cape Henrietta Maria. Canada. Geological Survey. Summary report, 1908, p. 93-94.

Paradis, C. A. M.
    De Temiskaming a la baie d'Hudson. Québec, 1900. vi, 78 p. illus.

Paradis, C. A. M.
    From Temiskaming to Hudson Bay. N. p. [1900] vi, 70 p. illus.

Parks, W. A.
    The Nipissing-Algoma boundary. Ontario. Department of Mines. Annual report, v. 8, p. 175-196. 1899. illus.

Peters, Austin
    James Bay adventure. Forest and outdoors,
v. 48, no. 5, p. 14-15, 28-29. May 1952. illus.

Proulx, J. B.
    A la baie d'Hudson; où, Récit de la première
visite pastorale de Mgr. N. Z. Lorrain. Montréal,
St. Joseph, 1886. 284 p. illus.

Proulx, J. B.
    En route pour la baie d'Hudson. Tours, Alfred
Mame, 1893. 157 p. illus.

Randall, Peter, and J. T. H. Johnson
    Abitibi holiday. Beaver, outfit 277, p. 34-36.
June 1946. illus.

Renison, R. J.
    One day at a time; autobiography. Toronto,
Kingswood House, 1957. 322 p. illus.

Roberts, Lloyd
    Land of romance; northern and north-western
Ontario. Canadian geographical journal, v. 18,
p. 114-145. 1939. illus.

Shearwood, M. H.
    By water and the Word; a transcript of the diary
of the Right Reverend J. A. Newnham. Toronto,
Macmillan, 1943. viii, 215 p. illus.

Société de Geographie de Québec
    Un voyage au pays des Cris. Société de geographie
de Québec. Bulletin, v. 17, p. 180-183. 1923.

Troyes, Pierre
    Journal de l'expedition du chevalier de troyes
a la baie d'Hudson, en 1686. Edité et annoté par
l'abbe Ivanhoe Caron. Beauceville, La Compagnie
de L'Eclaireur, 1918. ix, 136 p. map.

Umfreville, Edward
    The present state of Hudson's Bay. Containing a full description of that settlement and the adjacent country; and likewise of the fur trade, with hints for its improvement, &c. &c...London, printed for Charles Stalker, 1790. vii, 230 p. illus.

Williamson, O. T. G.
    Moosonee is threshold of true north magic. Saturday night, v. 63, p. 12-13. June 12, 1948.

Williamson, O. T. G.
    The northland Ontario. Toronto, Ryerson [1948] ix, 110 p. illus.

Wilson, A. W. G.
    A geological reconnaissance about the headwaters of the Albqny River. Canada. Geological Survey. Summary report, 1902, p. 201-206.

Wilson, A. W. G.
    James Bay exploration 1905; report of the geologist. Ontario. Northland Transportation Commission. Annual report, v. 4, p. 57-69. 1905. map.

Wilson, Clifford
    English River canoe trip. Beaver, outfit 279, p. 38-43. March 1949. illus., map.

Wilson, Clifford. See also Cotter, J. L. and Clifford Wilson

Wilson, W. J.
    The Little Current and Drowning Rivers, branches of the Albany, cast of Lake Nipigon. Canada. Geological Survey. Summary report, 1904, p. 164-173.

Wilson, W. J.
    Reconnaissance surveys of four rivers southwest of James Bay. Canada. Geological Survey. Summary report, 1902, p. 220-239. illus., map.

GEOGRAPHY

Adams, J. Q.
    Contrasting type of settlement on the James Bay plain. Scottish geographical magazine, v. 55, p. 212-217. 1939. illus., map.

Boucher, G. P. See Gosselin, A. and G. P. Boucher

Carruthers, Janet
    Land of the Ojibway. Beaver, outfit 282, p. 42-43. March 1952. illus.

Coates, D. F.
    Mapping the north; establishing the land control for aerial survey on James Bay. Canadian geographical journal, v. 43, p. 58-69. 1951. illus. map.

Coombs, D. B.
    The Hudson Bay lowland; a geographical study. Montreal, 1952. iv, 226 ℓ. illus., maps. (McGill University. M.A. thesis)

Coombs, D. B.
    The physiographic subdivisions of the Hudson Bay lowlands south of 60 degrees north. Geographical bulletin, no. 6, p. 1-16. 1954. illus., maps.

Dean, W. G.
    Human geography of the lower Albany River basin. Geographical bulletin, no. 10, p. 55-75. 1957. illus., maps.

Gardner, Gerard
    La region de la baie James. L'Actualité économique, v. 22, p. 220-260. 1946. map.

Gosselin, A. and G. P. Boucher
    Settlement problems in northwestern Quebec and northeastern Ontario. Ottawa King's Printer 1944. 54 p. map. (Canada. Department of Agriculture. Technical bulletin no. 49)

Hustich, Ilmari
    On the phytogeography of the subarctic Hudson Bay lowland. Helsinki, Societas Geographica Fenniae, 1957. 48 p. illus., maps. (Acta geographica, v. 16, no. 1)

Kindle, E. M.
    The James Bay coastal plain; notes on a journey. Geographical review, v. 15, p. 226-236. 1925. illus.

Langelier, J. C.
    Le bassin méridional de la baie d'Hudson. Québec, Joseph Dussault, 1887. 104 p.

* McDermott, G. L.
    Frontiers of settlement in the great clay belt, Ontario and Quebec. Association of American Geographers. Annals, v. 51, no. 3, p. 261-273. Sept. 1961.

Manning, T. H.
    Exploration of James and Hudson Bays, 1947. [Ottawa, Geodetic Service of Canada, 1948] 166 ℓ. map.

Moir, D. R.
    Beach ridges and vegetation in the Hudson Bay region. Proceedings of the North Dakota Academy of Science, v. 8, p. 45-48. 1954.

Moir, D. R.
    Land forms in the region south of Hudson Bay. [Fargo, N. D.? 1954?] 9 p.

Geography

Natural Resources, Canada
   Magnetic survey of Albany River. Natural resources, Canada, v. 9, no. 2, p. 2. Feb. 1930.

Nichols, D. A.
   The geographic setting of northern Ontario. Canadian geographical journal, v. 18, p. 147-151. 1939. illus.

Ogilvie, William
   Report of exploratory survey to Hudson's Bay. [Ottawa? 1891?] 26 p.

Richards, H. G.
   James Bay, "Canada's land of tomorrow". Bulletin of the Geographical Society of Philadelphia, v. 34, p. 27-32. 1936. illus., map.

Thorman, G. E.
   An early map of James Bay. Beaver, outfit 291, p. 18-22. Spring 1961. map.

SEE ALSO

McMillan, J. G.
   Investigations at James Bay during 1912
   METEOROLOGY

Moir, D. R.
   A floristic survey of the Severn River drainage basin of northwestern Ontario
   BOTANY

Ogilvie, N. J.
   The coast-line and islands of Hudson Bay
   METEOROLOGY

Smith, R. M.
   Northern Ontario
   ECONOMICS AND DEVELOPMENT

Sullivan, E. A. E.
    Engineer's report of exploration survey to James
  Bay
    TRANSPORTATION

GEOLOGY AND MINING

Adams, J. I.
    Laboratory compression tests on peat. Ontario hydro research quarterly, v. 14, no. 3, p. 35-40. July-September 1962. illus.

Armstrong, H. S.
    Geology of Echo township. Toronto, King's Printer, 1951. 40 p. illus., map. (Ontario. Department of Mines. Annual report, v. 59, pt. 5. 1950)

Baker, M. B.
    Iron and lignite in the Mattagami basin. Ontario. Department of Mines. Annual report, v. 20, pt. 1, p. 214-246. 1911. illus., map.

Bateman, J. D.
    Geology and gold deposits of the Uchi-Slate Lakes area. Ontario. Department of Mines. Annual report, v. 48, pt. 8, p. 1-43. 1939. illus., map.

Bateman, J. D.
    Geology at the J-M Consolidated mine. Ontario. Department of Mines. Annual report, v. 48, pt. 8, p. 44-52. 1939. illus.

Bateman, J. D.
    Geology of the North Spirit Lake area. Ontario. Department of Mines. Annual report, v. 47, pt. 7, p. 44-78. 1938. illus., maps.

Bateman, J. D.
    Recent developments in the Favourable Lake area. Ontario. Department of Mines. Annual report, v. 47, pt. 7, p. 79-92. 1938. illus., map.

Bell, J. M.
   Economic resources of Moose River basin.
Ontario. Department of Mines. Annual report,
v. 13, pt. 1, p. 135-179. 1904. illus.

Bell, Robert
   Proofs of the rising of the land around Hudson
Bay. American journal of science, ser. 4, v. 1,
p. 219-228. 1896.

Bell, Robert
   Report on the geology of the basin of Moose
River and of the Lake of the Woods and adjacent
country. Montreal, Dawson, 1883. 9 p. illus.,
map. (Canada. Geological Survey. Report of
progress, 1880-1882, pt. C)

Bell, Robert
   Rising of the land around Hudson Bay. Smithsonian Institute. Annual report to July 1897,
p. 359.

Bennett, G.   See Brown, D. D., G. Bennett and P. T.
George

Brown, D. D., G. Bennett and P. T. George
   The source of alluvial kimberlite indicator
minerals in the James Bay lowland. [Toronto]
Department of Mines, 1967. iv, 35 p. illus.
(Ontario. Department of Mines. Miscellaneous
paper MP. 7)

Bruce, E. L.
   Area south of the west end of Lake St. Joseph.
Ontario. Department of Mines. Annual report, v.
31, pt. 8, p. 39-40. 1922. map.

Bruce, E. L.
   Eastern part of Lake St. Joseph. Ontario.
Department of Mines. Annual report, v. 31, pt. 8,
p. 33-38. 1922. illus., map.

Bruce, E. L. and J. E. Hawley
    Geology of the basin of Red Lake, district of
Kenora (Patricia portion) Ontario. Department of
Mines. Annual report, v. 36, pt. 3, p. 1-72.
1927. illus., maps.

Bruce, E. L.
    Geology of the basin of Red Lake, district of
Patricia. Ontario. Department of Mines. Annual
report, v. 33, pt. 4, p. 12-39. 1924. illus.,
map.

Bruce, E. L.
    Geology of the upper part of the English River.
Ontario. Department of Mines. Annual report, v.
33, pt. 4, p. 1-11. 1924. map.

Bruce, E. L.
    Gold deposits of Woman, Narrow and Confederation
Lakes, district of Kenora (Patricia portion).
Ontario. Department of Mines. Annual report,
v. 37, pt. 4, p. 1-51. 1928. illus., map.

Bruce, E. L.
    Iron formation of Lake St. Joseph. Ontario.
Department of Mines. Annual report, v. 31, pt. 8,
p. 1-32. 1922. illus.

Burwash, E. M.
    Geology of the Fort Hope gold area, district
of Kenora (Patricia portion). Ontario. Department
of Mines. Annual report, v. 38, pt. 2, p. 1-48.
1929. illus., maps.

Canada. Geological Survey
    Summary report, 1919, pt. G. Ottawa, King's
Printer, 1920. 23 p. maps.

Carlson, H. D.
    Geology of the Werner Lake-Rex Lake area.
Toronto, Queen's Printer, 1958. iii, 30 p. illus.,

maps. (Ontario. Department of Mines. Annual report, v. 66, pt. 4. 1957)

Charlewood, G. H., comp.
   Geology of deep development on the main ore zone at Kirkland Lake. Toronto, Queen's Printer, 1964. vi, 49 p. illus. (Ontario. Department of Mines. Geological circular no. 11.)

Chisholm, E. O.
   Geology of Balmer township. Toronto, King's Printer, 1954. iv, 62 p. illus., maps. (Ontario. Department of Mines. Annual report v. 60, pt. 10. 1951)

Coleman, A. P.
   Lake Ojibway; last of the great glacial lakes. Ontario. Department of Mines. Annual report, v. 18, pt. 1, p. 284-293. 1909. map.

Coleman, A. P.
   The northern nickle range. Ontario. Department of Mines. Annual report, v. 13, pt. 1, p. 192-224. 1904. illus.

Collins, W. H.
   Explorations along the National Transcontinental Railway location from Sturgeon River westward. Canada. Geological Survey. Summary report, 1907, p. 48-54.

Collins, W. H.
   A geological reconnaissance of the region traversed by the National Transcontinental Railway between Lake Nipigon and Clay Lake, Ontario. Ottawa, Government Printing Bureau, 1909. 67 p. illus., maps. (Canada. Geological Survey. Report no. 1059)

Collins, W. H.
   On surveys along the National Transcontinental

Railway location between Lake Nipigon and Lac Seul.
Canada. Geological Survey. Summary report, 1906,
p. 103-109.

Collins, W. H.
    Report on a portion of northwestern Ontario
traversed by the National Transcontinental Railway
between Lake Nipigon and Sturgeon Lake. Ottawa,
King's Printer, 1908. 23 p. illus., map. (Canada.
Geological Survey. Report no. 992)

Cooke, H. C.
    Studies of the physiography of the Canadian
Shield. II. Glacial depression and post-glacial
uplift. Transactions of the Royal Society of
Canada, ser. 3, v. 24, sect. 4, p. 51-87. 1930.
maps.

Cooke, H. C.
    Studies of the physiography of the Canadian
Shield. III. The pre-Pliocene physiographies as
inferred from the geologic record. Transactions
of the Royal Society of Canada, ser. 3, v. 25,
sect. 4, p. 127-180. 1931.

Cross, J. G.
    Pre-Cambrian rocks and iron ore deposits in the
Abitibi-Mattagami area. Ontario. Department of
Mines. Annual report, v. 29, pt. 2, p. 1-18.
1920. illus., maps.

Crozier, A. R.
    Refractory clay deposits on the Missinaibi River.
Ontario. Department of Mines. Annual report,
v. 42, pt. 3, p. 88-101. 1933. illus., maps.

Crozier, A. R. See also Dyer, W. S. and A. R. Crozier

Davey, E. R.
    Tests on Onakawana fire clays. Journal of the
Canadian Ceramic Society, v. 1, p. 40-46. 1932.

Derry, D. R.
   Geology of the area from Minaki to Sydney Lake, district of Kenora. Ontario. Department of Mines. Annual report, v. 39, pt. 3, p. 24-41. 1930. illus., map.

Derry, D. R. and G. S. MacKenzie
   Geology of the Ontario-Manitoba boundary (12th base line to latitude 54) Ontario. Department of Mines. Annual report, v. 40, pt. 2, p. 1-20. 1931. illus., map.

Douglas, G. V.
   Reconnaissance from Red Lake to Favourable Lake, District of Patricia. Toronto, King's Printer, 1926. 28 p. illus. (Ontario. Department of Mines. Annual report, v. 35, pt. 4. 1925)

Dowling, D. B.
   Report on an exploration of Ekwan River, Sutton Mill Lakes and part of the west coast of James Bay. Ottawa, King's Printer, 1904. 60 p. illus. (Canada. Geological Survey. Annual report, n.s., v. 14, pt. F. 1901)

Dowling, D. B.
   Report on the country in the vicinity of Red Lake and part of the basin of Berens River, Keewatin. Ottawa, Queen's Printer, 1896. 54 p. map. (Canada. Geological Survey. Annual report, n. s., v. 7, pt. F. 1894)

Dyer, W. S.
   Fire clay deposits of the Moose River (geology and field notes). Journal of the Canadian Ceramic Society, v. 1, p. 32-39. 1952.

Dyer, W. S.
   Geology and economic deposits of the Moose River basin. Ontario. Department of Mines. Annual report, v. 37, pt. 6, p. 1-69. 1928. illus., maps.

Dyer, W. S.
    Geology of the Pashkokogan-Misehkow area.
  Ontario. Department of Mines. Annual report,
  v. 42, pt. 6, p. 1-20. 1933. illus., map.

Dyer, W. S. and A. R. Crozier
    Lignite and refractory clay deposits of the
  Onakawana lignite field. Ontario. Department of
  Mines. Annual report, v. 42, pt. 3, p. 46-87.
  1933. illus., map.

Dyer, W. S.
    The lignite deposit at Onakawana, Moose River
  basin, Ontario. Transactions of the Canadian
  Institute of Mining and Metallurgy, v. 33, p. 450-
  472. 1930. illus.

Dyer, W. S.
    Limestones of the Moose River and Albany River
  basins. Ontario. Department of Mines. Annual
  report, v. 38, pt. 4, p. 31-33. 1929.

Dyer, W. S.
    The Onakawana lignite deposit Moose River basin
  (Progress report to May 31, 1930). Ontario. Department of Mines. Annual report, v. 39, pt. 6, p. 1-
  14. 1930. illus., maps.

Dyer, W. S.
    Paleozoic geology of the Albany River and cer-
  tain of its tributaries. Ontario. Department of
  Mines. Annual report, v. 38, pt. 4, p. 47-60.
  1929. illus.

Dyer, W. S. and A. R. Crozier
    Refactory clays of northern Ontario. Trans-
  actions of the Canadian Institute of Mining and
  Metallurgy, v. 36, p. 238-252. 1933. illus.,
  maps.

Dyer, W. S.
    Stratigraphy and structural geology of the Moose

River basin, northern Ontario. Transactions of the Royal Society of Canada, ser. 3, v. 25, sect. 4, p. 85-99. 1931. map.

Edwards, B. G.
    Developing and operating a mine on the Canadian tundra. Canadian mining journal, v. 65, p. 135-146, 214-227, 300-312, 380-396, 467-478. March-July 1944. illus., map.

Evans, E. L.
    Geology of the eastern extension of Crow River area. Toronto, King's Printer, 1941. 7 p. illus., map. (Ontario. Department of Mines. Annual report, v. 48, pt. 7. 1939)

Flint, R. F.
    New radiocarbon dates and late-Pleistocene stratigraphy. American journal of science, v. 254, p. 265-287. May 1956. map.

Furse, G. D.
    Geology of the Shabumani-Birch Lakes area. Ontario. Department of Mines. Annual report, v. 42, pt. 6, p. 21-51. 1933. illus., maps.

George, P. T. See Brown, D. D., G. Bennett and P. T. George

Gilbert, Geoffrey
    Gammon River area and Bickaby Lake Schist belt, district of Kenora (Patricia portion). Ontario. Department of Mines. Annual report, v. 36, pt. 3, p. 73-84. 1927. map.

Gilchrist, Lachlan
    Investigations in the Onakawana lignite field, Abitibi River, Ontario. In his Geophysical investigation made in 1930. Canada. Geological Survey. Memoir no. 170, p. 92-98. 1932. illus.

Gilmore, R. E.
    Lignite coal from Blacksmith Rapids, Abitibi
River. Ontario. Department of Mines. Annual report, v. 38, pt. 4, p. 34-40. 1929.

Goodwin, A. M.
    Volcanic studies in the Birch-Uchi Lakes area
of Ontario. [Toronto] Department of Mines, 1967.
vi, 96 p. illus., map. (Ontario. Department
of Mines. Miscellaneous paper MP. 6)

Greig, J. W.
    Woman and Narrow Lakes area, district of Kenora
(Patricia portion). Ontario. Department of Mines.
Annual report, v. 36, pt. 3, p. 85-110. 1927.
illus., map.

Gussow, W. C.
    Geology of the Caribou-Pikitiqushi area.
Toronto, King's Printer, 1942. 12 p. map.
(Ontario. Department of Mines. Annual report,
v. 49, pt. 6. 1940)

Gussow, W. C.
    Silurian reefs of James Bay lowland, Ontario.
American Association of Petroleum Geologists.
Bulletin, v. 37, p. 2422-2424. 1953. illus.

Harding, W. D.
    Geology of the Birch-Springpole Lakes area.
Toronto, King's Printer, 1936. iii, 33 p. illus.,
maps. (Ontario. Department of Mines. Annual report, v. 45, pt. 4. 1936)

Harding, W. D.
    Geology of the Cat River-Kawinogans Lake area.
Ontario. Department of Mines. Annual report,
v. 44, pt. 6, p. 53-73. 1935. illus., maps.

Harding, W. D.
    Geology of the Gullwing Lake-Sunstrum area,
Ontario. Toronto, King's Printer, 1951. iii,

29 p. illus., map. (Ontario. Department of Mines. Annual report, v. 59, pt. 4. 1950)

Hawley, J. E.
 Geology and economic possibilities of Sutton Lake area, district of Patricia. Toronto, King's Printer, 1926. v, 56 p. illus., maps. (Ontario. Department of Mines. Annual report, v. 34, pt. 7. 1925)

Hawley, J. E. See also Bruce, E. L. and J. E. Hawley

Hopkins, P. E.
 Ogahalla to Collins on the National Transcontinental Railway, Ontario. Ontario. Department of Mines. Annual report, v. 27, pt. 1, p. 187-199. 1918. illus., maps.

Horwood, H. C.
 Geology and mineral deposits of the Red Lake area. Toronto, King's Printer, 1945. vii, 231 p. illus., maps. (Ontario. Department of Mines. Annual report, v. 49, pt. 2. 1940)

Horwood, H. C.
 Geology at the Darkwater mine. Ontario. Department of Mines. Annual report, v. 46, pt. 6, p. 26-35. 1937. illus., maps.

Horwood, H. C.
 Geology of the Casummit Lake area and the Argosy mine. Toronto, King's Printer, 1938. iii, 33 p. illus., maps. (Ontario. Department of Mines. Annual report, v. 46, pt. 7. 1937)

Horwood, H. C.
 Geology of the Superior Junction-Sturgeon Lake area. Ontario. Department of Mines. Annual report, v. 46, pt. 6, p. 1-25. 1937. illus., maps.

Hudec, P. P. See Williamson, W. R. M. and P. P. Hudec

Geology and Mining

Hughes, O. L.
    Surficial geology of Smooth Rock, Cochrane district, Ontario. Ottawa [Queen's Printer?] 1956. 9 p. map. (Canada. Geological Survey. Paper 55-41)

Hughes, O. L. See also Terasmae, Jaan and O. L. Hughes

Hurst, M. R.
    Geology of the area between Favourable Lake and Sandy Lake, district of Kenora (Patricia portion) Ontario. Department of Mines. Annual report, v. 38, pt. 2, p. 49-84. 1929. illus., map.

Hurst, M. E.
    Geology of the Sioux Lookout area. Ontario. Department of Mines. Annual report, v. 41, pt. 6, p. 1-33. 1932. illus., map.

Hurst, M. E.
    Gold deposits in the vicinity of Red Lake. Ontario. Department of Mines. Annual report, v. 44, pt. 6, p. 1-52. 1935. illus., maps.

Hurst, M. E.
    Pickle Lake-Crow River area, district of Kenora (Patricia portion) Ontario. Department of Mines. Annual report, v. 39, pt. 2, p. 1-35. 1950. illus., maps.

Johnson, J. P.
    Meridian and base lines south of Lake St. Joseph, district of Thunder Bay. Ontario. Department of Mines. Annual report, v. 33, pt. 6, p. 40-48. 1924. illus.

Keele, Joseph
    Clay and shale deposits of the Abitibi and Mattagami Rivers. Ontario. Department of Mines. Annual report, v. 29, pt. 2, p. 31-55. 1920. illus.

Keele, Joseph
    Mesozoic clays and sands in northern Ontario.
Transactions of the Royal Society of Canada, ser.
3, v. 15, sect. 4, p. 25-46. 1921.

Keele, Joseph
    Mesozoic clays and sands in northern Ontario.
Canada. Geological Survey. Summary report, 1920,
pt. D, p. 35-39. map.

Keele, Joseph
    Mesozoic clays an northern Ontario. Canada.
Geological Survey. Summary report, 1919, pt. G,
p. 13-23.

Keele, Joseph
    Notes on clays of the Missinaibi River. Ontario.
Department of Mines. Annual report, v. 30, pt. 1,
p. 171-175. 1921. illus.

Keele, Joseph
    Notes on clays of the Missinaibi River. Ontario.
Department of Mines. Annual report, v. 31, pt. 10,
p. 95-96. 1922.

Kindle, E. M.
    Geology of a portion of the northern part of
Moose River basin, Ontario. Canada. Geological
Survey. Summary report, 1923, pt. C1, p. 21-41.
illus.

Laird, H. C.
    Geology of the Shonia Lake area, district of
Kenora (Patricia portion). Ontario. Department
of Mines. Annual report, v. 39, pt. 3, p. 1-23.
1930. illus., maps.

Langford, F. F.
    Geology of the Gripp Lake area. Toronto, King's
Printer, 1958. iii, 22 p. illus., map. (Ontario.
Department of Mines. Annual report, v. 67, pt. 3.
1958)

La Rocque, A.
    Post-Pleistocene connection between James Bay and the Gulf of Saint Lawrence. Bulletin of the Geological Society of America, v. 60, p. 363-379. 1949. maps.

Lee, H. A.
    Late glacial and postglacial Hudson Bay Sea episode. Science, v. 131, p. 1609-1611. 1960. illus.

Leith, C. K.
    An Algonkian basin in Hudson Bay - a comparison with the Lake Superior basin. Economic geology, v. 5, p. 227-246. 1910. map.

Low, A. P.
    Preliminary report on an exploration of country between Lake Winnipeg and Hudson Bay. Montreal, Dawson, 1887. 24 p. (Canada. Geological Survey. Annual report, n. s., v. 2, pt. F. 1886)

McInnes, William
    The headwaters of the Winish and Attawapiskat Rivers. Canada. Geological Survey. Summary report, 1905, p. 76-80.

McInnes, William
    The upper parts of the Winisk and Attawapiskat Rivers. Canada. Geological Survey. Summary report, 1904, p. 153-160.

MacKenzie, G. S. See Derry, D. R. and G. S. MacKenzie

McLearn, F. H.
    The Mesozoic and Pleistocene deposits of the lower Missinaibi, Opazatika, and Mattagami Rivers, Ontario. Canada. Geological Survey. Summary report. 1926, pt. C, p. 16-44. illus., map.

Malcolm, Wyatt
    Limestone on Abitibi and Mattagami Rivers,
Ontario. Canada. Geological Survey. Summary
report, 1924, pt. C, p. 96-98. map.

Martison, N. W.
    Petroleum possibilities of the James Bay lowland
area. Ontario. Department of Mines. Annual report, v. 61, pt. 6, p. 1-113. 1952. illus., maps.

Meen, V. B.
    Geology of the Sachigo River area. Ontario.
Department of Mines. Annual report, v. 46, pt. 4,
p. 32-59. 1937. illus., map.

Montgomery, R. J. and R. J. Watson
    Fire clay, kaolin and silica sand deposits of
the Mattagami and Missinaibi Rivers. Ontario.
Department of Mines. Annual report, v. 37, pt.
6, p. 80-120. 1928. illus., maps.

Montgomery, R. J.
    Testing of fire brick made from Mattagami River
fire clay. Ontario. Department of Mines. Annual
report, v. 39, pt. 6, p. 15-21. 1930. illus.

Moore, E. S.
    Iron range north of Round Lake. Ontario.
Department of Mines. Annual report, v. 18, pt. 1,
p. 154-162. 1909. illus.

Moore, E. S.
    Lake Savant area, district of Thunder Bay.
Ontario. Department of Mines. Annual report,
v. 37, pt. 4, p. 53-82. 1928. illus., map.

Moore, E. S.
    Lake Savant iron range area. Ontario. Department of Mines. Annual report, v. 19, pt. 1, p. 173-192. 1910.

Geology and Mining 73

Moorhouse, W. W.
    Geology of the O'Sullivan Lake area. Toronto, King's Printer, 1956. iii, 32 p. illus., maps. (Ontario. Department of Mines. Annual report, v. 64, pt. 4. 1955)

Ontario. Department of Mines
    Geology of Ontario-Manitoba boundary. Toronto, King's Printer, 1923. 64 p. illus., maps. (Its Annual report, v. 32, pt. 2. 1923)

Ontario. Department of Mines
    Investigations of non-metallic mineral resources of Ontario, 1929. Toronto, King's Printer, 1931. 65 p. illus. (Its Annual report, v. 39, pt. 6. 1930)

Ontario. Department of Mines.
    Investigations of non-metallic mineral resources of Ontario, 1928. Toronto, King's Printer, 1930. 67 p. illus., maps. (Its Annual report, v. 38, pt. 4. 1929)

Ontario Research Foundation
    A technical and economic investigation of northern Ontario lignite. Ontario. Department of Mines. Annual report, v. 42, pt. 3, p. 1-45. 1933. illus., map.

Parks, W. A.
    The Huronian of the Moose River basin. Toronto, University Library, 1900. 35 p. map. (University of Toronto studies. Geological series, no. 1)

Parks, W. A.
    Region lying north-east of Lake Nipigon. Canada. Geological Survey. Summary report, 1902, p. 211-220.

Pettijohn, F. J.
    Conglomerate of Abram Lake, Ontario, and its extensions. Bulletin of the Geological Society of

America, v. 45, p. 479-505. 1934. illus., maps.

Potter, David
    Botanical evidence of a post-Pleistocene marine connection between Hudson Bay and the St. Lawrence basin. Rhodora, v. 34, p. 68-89, 101-112. 1932. maps.

Prest, V. K.
    Geology of the eastern extension of the Fort Hope area. Ontario. Department of Mines. Annual report, v. 51, pt. 3, p. 29-39. 1942. illus., map.

Prest, V. K.
    Geology of the Fort Hope area. Ontario. Department of Mines. Annual report, v. 51, pt. 3, p. 1-28. 1942. illus., map.

Prest, V. K.
    Geology of the Keeshik-Miminiska Lakes area. Toronto, King's Printer, 1939. 17 p. illus., map. (Ontario. Department of Mines. Annual report, v. 48, pt. 6. 1939)

Prest, V. K.
    Red Lake-Lansdowne House area, northwestern Ontario; surficial geology. [Ottawa] Department of Mines and Technical Surveys [1963] 23 p. maps. (Canada. Geological Survey. Paper 63-6)

Prest, V. K.
    Geology of the Rowlandson Lake area. Ontario. Department of Mines. Annual report, v. 49, pt. 8, p. 1-9. 1940. illus., map.

Prest, V. K.
    Geology of the Wunnummin Lake area. Ontario. Department of Mines. Annual report, v. 49, pt. 8, p. 10-19. 1940. illus., map.

Geology and Mining

Rittenhouse, Gordon
    Geology of a portion of the Savant Lake area,
    Ontario. Journal of geology, v. 44, p. 451-478.
    1936. maps.

Rogers, W. R.
    District of Patricia, Red Lake and adjacent
    areas. Toronto, King's Printer, 1926. 11 p.
    maps. (Ontario. Department of Mines. Bulletin
    no. 56)

Roliff, W. A.
    Exploration for oil and gas in eastern Canada.
    Proceedings of the Geological Association of Canada,
    v. 7, pt. 1, p. 61-81. 1955. maps.

[Satterly, Jack and others]
    Drilling in the James Bay lowland. Ontario.
    Department of Mines. Annual report, v. 61, pt. 6,
    p. 115-157. 1952.

Satterly, Jack
    Geology of the Sandy Lake area. Ontario.
    Department of Mines. Annual report, v. 47, pt. 7,
    p. 1-43. 1938. illus., maps.

Satterly, Jack
    Geology of the Stull Lake area. Ontario.
    Department of Mines. Annual report, v. 46, pt. 4,
    p. 1-32. 1937. illus., maps.

Satterly, Jack
    Geology of the Windigo-North Caribou Lakes
    area. Toronto, King's Printer, 1940. 32 p.
    illus., maps. (Ontario. Department of Mines.
    Annual report, v. 48, pt. 9. 1939)

Satterly, Jack
    Glacial lakes Ponask and Sachigo, district of
    Kenora, Ontario. Journal of Geology, v. 45, p.
    790-796. 1937. illus., map.

Satterly, Jack
    Pleistocene glaciation in the Windigo-North Caribou Lakes area, Kenora district, Ontario. Transactions of the Royal Canadian Institute, v. 23, pt. 1, p. 75-82. 1940. illus., map.

Savage, T. E.
    Correlation of the early Silurian rocks in the Hudson Bay region. Journal of geology, v. 26, p. 334-340. 1918.

Savage, T. E. and F. M. Van Tuyl
    Geology and stratigraphy of the area of Paleozoic rocks in the vicinity of Hudson and James Bays. Bulletin of the Geological Society of America, v. 30, p. 339-377. 1919. illus., maps.

Savage, T. E. and F. M. Van Tuyl
    The University of Illinois Hudson Bay expedition. Science, v. 44, p. 632. 1916.

Terasmae, Jaan
    Contributions to Canadian palynology, part III; non-glacial deposits along Missinaibi River, Ontario. Canada. Geological Survey. Bulletin 46, p. 29-35. 1958.

Terasmae, Jaan
    Paleobotanical studies of Canadian pleistocene nonglacial deposits. Science, v. 126, no. 3269, p. 351-352. August 23, 1957.

Terasmae, Jaan and O. L. Hughes
    A palynological and geological study of Pleistocene deposits in the James Bay lowlands, Ontario (42 N½) [Ottawa, Queen's Printer, 1960] ix, 15 p. illus., map. (Canada. Geological Survey. Bulletin 62)

Thomson, J. E.
    The Crow River area. Ontario. Department of

Mines. Annual report, v. 47, pt. 3, p. 1-65. 1938.
illus., maps.

Thomson, J. E.
   The Uchi Lake area. Ontario. Department of
Mines. Annual report, v. 47, pt. 3, p. 66-82.
1938. illus., maps.

Thomson, Robert
   Geology of the Burntbush River area. Ontario.
Department of Mines. Annual report, v. 45, pt. 6,
p. 49-63. 1936. illus., map.

Tyrrell, J. B.
   Hudson Bay Exploring Expedition, 1912. Ontario.
Department of Mines. Annual report, v. 22, pt. 1,
p. 161-209. 1913. illus., maps.

Tyrrell, J. B.
   The Patrician glacier south of Hudson Bay.
Congrès Géologique International. 12th, Toronto.
1913. Compte-rendu, p. 523-534. map.

Van Tuyl, F. M. See Savage, T. E. and F. M. Van Tuyl

Watson, R. J. See Montgomery, R. J. and R. J. Watson

Webster, A. R.
   Hydro-electric development for the mining
industry of northern Ontario. Toronto, King's
printer, 1930. 31 p. illus., maps. (Ontario.
Department of Mines. Bulletin no. 46, rev. ed.
April 1930)

Williams, M. Y.
   Palaeozoic rocks of Mattagami and Abitibi Rivers.
Canada. Geological Survey. Summary report, 1919,
pt. G. p. 1-12. maps.

Williams, M. Y.
   Palaeozoic stratigraphy of Pagwachuan, lower

Kenogami, and lower Albany Rivers. Canada. Geological Survey. Summary report, 1920, pt. D, p. 18-25. map.

Williams, M. Y.
    Paleozoic geology of the Mattagami and Abitibi Rivers. Ontario. Department of Mines. Annual report, v. 29, pt. 2, p. 19-30. 1920. illus.

Williamson, W. R. M. and P. P. Hudec
    Geology of the Wapesi Lake-Tully Lake area. Toronto, King's Printer, 1959. 11 p. illus., map. (Ontario. Department of Mines. Annual report, v. 67, pt. 4. 1958)

Wilson, A. W. G.
    Report on a traverse through the southern Part of the Northwest Territories from Lac Seul to Cat Lake in 1902. Ottawa, Government Printing Bureau, 1909. 25 p. (Canada. Geological Survey. Report no. 1006)

Wilson, W. J.
    Geological reconnaissance of a portion of Algoma and Thunder Bay district. Ottawa, King's Printer, 1909. 49 p. illus. (Canada. Geological Survey. Report no. 980)

Wilson, W. J.
    The Nagagami River and other branches of the Kenogami. Canada. Geological Survey. Summary report, 1903, p. 109-120.

Zoltai, S. C.
    Glacial history of part of northwestern Ontario. Proceedings of the Geological Association of Canada, v. 13, p. 61-83. 1961. maps.

Geology and Mining

SEE ALSO

Douglass, D. P.
    Hydro-electric development for the mining industry of northern Ontario
    ECONOMICS AND DEVELOPMENT

Duffell, S., A. S. MacLaren and R. H. C. Holman
    Red Lake-Lansdowne House area
    ECONOMICS AND DEVELOPMENT

Duffell, S.
    "Roads to resources"
    ECONOMICS AND DEVELOPMENT

Enright, C. T.
    The muskeg factor in the location and construction of an Ontario Hydro service road in the Moose River basin
    ECONOMICS AND DEVELOPMENT

HISTORY

Arthur, E. R., Howard Chapman and Hart Massey
    Moose Factory, 1673 to 1947. I History II
Men in charge III Architecture IV Plates. Toronto, printed for the authors at the University of Toronto Press, 1949. 16 p. illus., map.

Belleau, Henri
    Les missions de la baie James. L'Apostolat, v. 11, p. 46-56. 1940. illus.

Beveridge, Thomas
    An account of the first mission of the Associate Synod of Canada West; transcribed and annotated by A. W. Taylor. Ontario history, v. 50, p. 101-111. 1958.

Boon, T. C. B.
    Moose mission on James Bay. Canadian churchman, v. 78, p. 218-219. 1951. illus.

Carrière, Gaston
    Les missions catholiques dans l'Est du Canada et l'honorable Compagnie de la baie d'Hudson (1844-1900). Revue de l'Université d'Ottawa, v. 27, p. 82-131, 220-266, 340-388. 1957.

Chapman, Howard. See Arthur, E. R., Howard Chapman and Hart Massey

Gibbon, M. E.
    Sacred to the memory. Beaver, outfit 287, p. 50-55. Spring 1957. illus.

Lyon-Fellowes, Evelyn
    Bridge building on the Pagwachnan. Ontario

History 81

    history, v. 54, p. 191-198. 1962.

Macfie, John
    Fawn River - an early fur trade route. Sylva,
v. 9, p. 3-7. Jan.-Feb. 1953. illus.

Marwick, Alice
    Northland post; the story of the town of Cochrane. Cochrane, Ontario [1950] 341 p. illus., map.

Massey, Hart. See Arthur, E. R., Howard Chapman and Hart Massey

Mathews, R. K.
    Albany - pawn in Anglo-French conflict. Beaver, outfit 297, p. 49-55. Autumn 1966. maps.

* Moccasin Telegraph. v. 1, no. 1- Aug. 1941-

* Moosonee Mailbag [later Moosonee and Keewatin Mailbag] and the Bishop's Annual Letter. v. 1, no. 1-[?] Oct. 1897-Oct. 1920.

* Northland. v. 1, no. 1- June 1944-

Pain, S. A.
    The way north; men, mines and minerals, being some account of the curious history of the ancient route between North Bay and Hudson Bay in Ontario. Toronto, Ryerson [c1964] 249 p. map.

Paul-Emile (Soeur Louise Mary Guay). Amiskwaski, la terre du castor. See Paul-Emile (Soeur Louise Mary Guay). La baie James; trois cents ans d'histoire militaire, economique, missionaire.

Paul-Emile (Soeur Louise Mary Guay)
    La baie James; trois cents ans d'histoire militaire, economique, missionaire. Ottawa, Université d'Ottawa [1952] 313 p. illus., maps.

Rich, E. E., ed.
    Moose Fort journals, 1783-85. London, Hudson's
Bay Record Society, 1954. xxx, 392 p. maps.
(Hudson's Bay Record Society. Publication 17)

Saindon, Emile
    En missionant: essai sur les missions des Pères
Oblats de Marie Immaculée à la baie James. Ottawa,
Imprimerie du droit, 1928. 79 p. illus.

Tyrrell, J. B.
    Arrivals and departures of ships
        TRANSPORTATION

Vollmer, Margaret
    Flying Santa Claus. Beaver, outfit 280, p. 40-
43. Dec. 1949. illus., map.

Zaslow, Morris
    Rendezvous at Moose Factory, 1882, with intro.
and notes. Ontario history, v. 53, p. 81-94.
June 1961. illus.

ICHTHYOLOGY

Bajkov, Alexander
    A preliminary report on the fishes of the
Hudson Bay drainage system. Canadian field-
naturalist, v. 42, p. 96-99. April 1928.

Bean, T. H.
    Notes on some fishes from Hudson Bay. Proceed-
ings of the United States National Museum, v. 4,
p. 127-129. 1881.

Crossman, E. J. See Ryder, R. A., W. B. Scott and
    E. J. Crossman

Dymond, J. R. and W. B. Scott
    Fishes of Patricia portion of the Kenora
district, Ontario. Copeia, 1941, p. 243-245.

Lower, A. R. M.
    A report on the fish and fisheries of the west
coast of James Bay. In Canada. Department of the
Naval Service. Reports on fisheries investigations
in Hudson and James Bays and tributary waters in
1914. Ottawa, King's Printer, 1915. p. 29-67.
illus., maps.

Ryder, R. A.
    First Ontario record of the arctic char,
Salvelinus alpinus. Copeia, 1961, p. 359-360.

Ryder, R. A., W. B. Scott and E. J. Crossman
    Fishes of northern Ontario, north of the Albany
River. [Toronto, printed for the Royal Ontario
Museum at the University of Toronto Press, 1964]
30 p. maps. (Royal Ontario Museum. Life Sciences.
Contribution no. 60)

Scott, W. B.   See Dymond, J. R. and W. B. Scott

Scott, W. B.   See Ryder, R. A., W. B. Scott and E. J. Crossman

SEE ALSO

Williams, M. Y.
    Notes on the fauna of lower Pagwachuan, lower Kenogami, and lower Albany Rivers of Ontario.
    MAMMALOGY

Williams, M. Y.
    Notes on the fauna of the Moose River and the Mattagami and Abitibi tributaries.
    MAMMALOGY

INVERTEBRATE ZOOLOGY

Baker, F. C. and A. R. Cahn
    Freshwater mollusca from Central Ontario.
Canada. National Museum. Bulletin no. 67,
p. 41-64. illus.

Cahn, A. R. See Baker, F. C. and A. R. Cahn

Goodrich, Calvin
    Mollusks of Moose Factory. Nautilus, v. 47,
p. 7-9. 1933.

Kurata, T. B.
    Two new species of Ontario spiders. Toronto,
University of Toronto Press, 1944. 6 p. illus.
(Royal Ontario Museum of Zoology. Occasional
papers, no. 8)

La Rocque, A.
    Lasmigona compressa (Lea) in the Hudson Bay
drainage. Canadian field-naturalist, v. 50,
p. 51-52. 1956.

[Latchford, F. R.]
    Conchological notes. Ottawa naturalist, v. 29,
p. 51-52. 1915.

Reed, E. B.
    Two new species of *Diaptomus* from arctic and
subarctic Canada (Calanoida, Copepoda). Canadian
journal of zoology, v. 36, p. 663-670. 1958.
illus.

Richards, H. G.
    Land and freshwater mollusks collected on a
trip to James Bay. Canadian field-naturalist,
v. 50, p. 58-60. 1936.

Whiteaves, J. F.
    List of land and fresh-water shells from the
district of Keewatin, collected by Mr. Wm. McInnes
in 1904. Canada. Geological Survey. Summary
report, 1904, p. 160-164.

Whiteaves, J. F.
    Lists of a few species of land and fresh-water
shells from the immediate vicinity of James Bay,
Hudson Bay. Nautilus, v. 19, p. 4. 1905.

Whiteaves, J. F.
    List of some fresh-water shells from north-
western Ontario and Keewatin. Canadian field-
naturalist, v. 20, p. 29-32. 1906.

Whiteaves, J. F.
    Notes on some freshwater and land shells from
Keewatin, Northern Ontario and British Columbia.
Ottawa naturalist, v. 16, p. 91-93. 1902.

LINGUISTICS

Adam, Lucien
    Esquisse d'une grammaire comparée de la langue des Chippeways et de la langue des Crees. Proceedings of the 1st International Congress of Americanists, v. 2, p. 88-148. 1875.

Bloomfield, Leonard
    Algonquian. In Hoijer, Harry, ed. Linguistic structures of native America. Viking Fund publications in anthropology, no. 6, 1946. p. 85-129.

Bloomfield, Leonard
    On the sound system of central Algonquian. Language, v. 1, p. 130-156. 1925.

Chamberlain, A. F.
    Cree and Ojibwa literary terms. Journal of American folklore, v. 19, p. 346-347. 1906.

Ellis, C. D.
    A note on Okima.kna.n: the role of the chief as seen through Cree eyes. Anthropological linguistics, v. 2, no. 3, p. 1. 1960.

Ellis, C. D.
    The so-called interrogative order in Cree. International journal of American linguistics, v. 27, no. 2, p. 119-124. 1961.

Ellis, C. D.
    Spoken Cree: west coast of James Bay. Toronto, Dept. of Missions, The Anglican Church of Canada, 1962- v.1-

Ellis, C. D.
    Tagmemic analysis of a restricted Cree text.
    Journal of the Canadian linguistic association,
    v. 6, no. 1, p. 35-59. 1960.

Faries, R., ed.
    A dictionary of the Cree language as spoken by
    the Indians in Quebec, Ontario, Manitoba, Saskat-
    chewan, and Alberta, based upon the foundations
    laid by the Rev. E. A. Watkins. Toronto, General
    Synod of the Church of England in Canada, 1938.
    ix, 530 p.

* Horden, J. A.
    A grammar of the Cree language. London, Society
    for Promoting Christian Knowledge. 1881. viii,
    238 p.

Horden, J. A.
    A grammar of the Cree language. Rev. ed. in
    plain Cree. London, Society for Promoting Christ-
    ian Knowledge, 1913. 209 p.

Hunter, James
    A lecture on the grammatical construction of the
    Cree language, delivered by the Ven. Archdeacon
    Hunter...before the Institute of Reupert's Land...
    Also paradigms of the Cree verb, with its various
    conjugations, moods, tenses, inflections, etc.
    London, Society for Promoting Christian Knowledge,
    1875. 267 p.

* Lendrum, Frank
    Moosonee place-names and their origin. The
    quarterly [Ontario Northland Railway] no. 62, p. 7-
    11. Sept., 1961.

Logan, R. A.
    The precise speakers. Beaver, outfit 282,
    p. 40-43. June, 1951.

Linguistics

* Logan, R. A.
    The Cree language as it appears to me. Lake
  Charlotte, N.S., Loganda, 1958. 37 p.

* Logan, R. A.
    Cree language notes. Lake Charlotte, N.S.,
  Loganda, 1958. 14 p.

Michelson, Truman
    Indian language studies on James and Hudson's
  Bays, Canada. Explorations and field work of the
  Smithsonian Institution, 1935. (Smithsonian
  Institution publication no. 3382, p. 75-80. 1936)

Michelson, Truman
    A report on a linguistic expedition to James
  and Hudson's Bays. American anthropologist, v. 38,
  no. 4, p. 685-686. 1936.

Rogers, J. H.
    Survey of Round Lake Ojibwa phonology and
  morphology. Canada. National Museum. Bulletin
  194, p. 92-154. 1964.

Saindon, J. E.
    Two Cree songs from James Bay. Primitive man,
  v. 7, no. 1, p. 6-7. 1934.

Tyrrell, J. B.
    Algonquian Indian names of places in northern
  Canada. Royal Canadian Institute. Transactions,
  v. 10, no. 2, p. 213-231. 1915.

Watkins, E. A., comp.
    A dictionary of the Cree languages as spoken by
  the Indians of the Hudson's Bay Company's territories. London, Society for Promoting Christian
  Knowledge, 1865. xxiv, 460 p.

Watkins, E. A. See also Faries, R.

MAMMALOGY

Barnston, George
    Observations on the progress of the seasons as affecting animals and vegetables at Martin's Falls, Albany River, Hudson's Bay. Edinburgh new philosophical journal, v. 30, p. 252-256. 1841.

Churcher, C. S.
    Mammals at Fort Albany circa 1700 AD. Journal of mammalogy, v. 46, p. 354-355. 1965.

Downing, S. C.
    First Ontario record of the subgenus *Mictomys*. Canadian field-naturalist, v. 54, p. 109-110. 1940.

Dymond, J. R.
    The northern limit of the white-railed deer in Ontario. Canadian field-naturalist, v. 44, p. 96. 1930.

Elton, C. S. and others
    The snowshoe rabbit inquiry, 1931-32 to 1942-43. Canadian field-naturalist, v. 47, p. 67-69, 84-86; v. 48, p. 73-78; v. 49, p. 79-85; v. 50, p. 71-81; v. 51, p. 63-73; v. 52, p. 63-72; v. 53, p. 63-70; v. 54, p. 117-124; v. 56, p. 17-21; v. 57, p. 64-68, 136-141; v. 60, p. 67-70. 1933-1943.

Forster, J. R.
    Account of several quadrupeds from Hudson's Bay. Royal Society of London. Philosophical transactions, v. 62, p. 370-381. 1772.

Munday, Albert
    Salvation of our beaver. Canadian geographical journal, v. 18, p. 341-345. June 1939. illus.

Preble, E. A.
    A biological investigation of the Hudson Bay
    region. Washington, Government Printing Office,
    1902. 140 p. illus., map. (U. S. Fish and
    Wildlife Survey. North American fauna, no. 22)

Williams, M. Y.
    Notes on the fauna of lower Paguachuan, lower
    Kenogami, and lower Albany Rivers of Ontario.
    Canadian field-naturalist, v. 35, p. 94-98. 1921.

Williams, M. Y.
    Notes of the fauna of the Moose River and the
    Mattagami and Abitibi tributaries. Canadian
    field-naturalist, v. 34, p. 121-126. 1920. map.

SEE ALSO

Rogers, E. S.
    A cursory examination of the fur returns from
    three Indian bands of northern Ontario
    ECONOMICS AND DEVELOPMENT.

MEDICINE

Arctic Circular
    Tuberculosis survey: James and Hudson Bays, 1950. Arctic circular, v. 4, p. 43-47. 1951.

Millar, John
    Tularaemia in northwestern Ontario. Journal of the Canadian Medical Association, v. 69, p. 102-105. Aug. 1953. illus.

Ramsay, George
    Towards Hudson Bay. Journal of the Canadian Medical Association, v. 58, p. 614-616. 1948.

Ridley, Frank
    An early patent medicine of the Canadian north. Canadian geographical journal, v. 73, p. 24-27. 1966. illus.

Robertson, E. C. See Tisdall, F. F. and E. C. Robertson

Tisdall, F. F. and E. C. Robertson
    Voyage of the medicine men. Beaver, outfit 279, p. 42-46. Dec. 1948. illus.

Vivian, R. P., and others
    The nutrition and health of the James Bay Indian. Journal of the Canadian Medical Association, v. 59, p. 505-518. 1948. illus.

METEOROLOGY

Allington, K. R., B. W. Boville and F. K. Hare
    Midwinter ozone variations and stratospheric flow over Canada, 1958-1959. Tellus, v. 12, p. 266-273. 1960. illus.

Boville, B. W. See Allington, K. R., B. W. Boville and F. K. Hare

Chapman, L. J.
    The climate of northern Ontario. Canadian journal of agricultural science, v. 33, p. 41-73. 1953. illus., maps.

Godson, W. L.
    The representation and analysis of vertical distributions of ozone. Quarterly journal of the Royal Meteorological Society, v. 88, p. 220-232. 1962. illus.

Hare, F. K.
    Climate and zonal divisions of the boreal forest formation in Eastern Canada. Geographical review, v. 40, p. 615-635. 1950. illus., maps.

Hare, F. K. See also Allington, K. R., B. W. Boville and F. K. Hare

Ireton, H. J. C. See McLennan, J. C., H. S. Wynne-Edwards and H. J. C. Ireton

Komhyr, W. D. and R. F. Sturrock
    Canadian measurements of relative ozone absorption coefficients with the Dobson spectrophotometer. International Union of Geodesy and Geophysics.

Monograph no. 3, p. 24. 1960.

Komhyr, W. D.
    Measurements of atmospheric ozone at Moosonee, Canada, July 1, 1957 to July 31, 1960. Toronto, 1961. 14 p. [+ 76 p. tables] (Canada. Department of Transport. Meteorological Branch. Canadian meteorological memoirs, no. 6)

Maher, W. R. See McMillan, J. G.

McLennan, J. C., H. S. Wynne-Edwards and H. J. C. Ireton
    Height of the polar aurora in Canada. Canadian journal of research, v. 5, p. 285-296. 1931. illus., maps.

McMillan, J. G.
    Investigations at James Bay during 1912 and Reconnaissance for extension by W. R. Maher. Toronto, King's Printer, 1913. 85 p. illus. (Temiskaming and Northern Ontario Railway. Report no. 3)

Ogilvie, N. J.
    The coast-line and islands of Hudson Bay – an ideal field for geodetic astronomical work. Transactions of the American Geophysical Union, v. 15, p. 41-45. 1934.

Sturrock, R. F. See Komhyr, W. D. and R. F. Sturrock

Wynne-Edwards, H. S. See McLennan, J. C., H. S. Wynne-Edwards and H. J. C. Ireton

MOOSE FACTORY AND MOOSONEE

SEE

Adams, J. Q.
    Contrasting type of settlement on the James
  Bay plain
    GEOGRAPHY

Canadian Transportation
    Moosonee
    TRANSPORTATION

Canadian Weekly Bulletin
    Ocean port at Moosonee
    TRANSPORTATION

Cotter, J. L. and Clifford Wilson
    Moose Factory
    GENERAL

Crooks, G. E.
    James Bay public library
    ECONOMICS AND DEVELOPMENT

Gibbon, M. E.
    Sacred to the memory
    HISTORY

Gibbon, M. E.
    Trapper's wife
    ETHNOLOGY

Goodrich, Calvin
    Mollusks of Moose Factory
    INVERTEBRATE ZOOLOGY

Langford, C. J.
   Moose River and its approaches
   TRANSPORTATION

Leitch, Adelaide
   Road to Moosonee
   GENERAL

Macfie, John
   Fawn River
   HISTORY

Mackay, Hugh
   Moose Factory
   GENERAL

Mawdsey-Jones, R. H. and C. Erentz
   Moosonee now hinted door to outer space
   ECONOMICS AND DEVELOPMENT

Monetary Times
   Opening of Moosonee port would double population of northeastern Ontario
   ECONOMICS AND DEVELOPMENT

Montgomery, Paul
   Ontario's newest north
   ECONOMICS AND DEVELOPMENT

Northeastern Ontario Development Association
   A report on the possible effects of a seaport at Moosonee on the economy of northeastern Ontario
   ECONOMICS AND DEVELOPMENT

Rae, John
   Notes on some of the birds and mammals of the Hudson's Bay Company's territory and of the arctic coast of America
   ORNITHOLOGY

Rich, E. E., ed.
    Moose Fort journal
    HISTORY

Tyrrell, J. B.
    Arrivals and departures of ships
    TRANSPORTATION

Williamson, O. T. G.
    Development of Moosonee as an ocean port
    TRANSPORTATION

Williamson, O. T. G.
    Moosonee
    TRANSPORTATION

Williamson, O. T. G.
    Moosonee is threshold of true north magic
    GENERAL

Zaslow, Morris
    Rendezvous at Moose Factory
    HISTORY

ORNITHOLOGY

Baillie, J. L.
   Four additional breeding birds of Ontario.
Canadian field-naturalist, v. 53, p. 130-131.
1939.

Baillie, J. L.
   On the spring flights of blue and snow geese
across northern Ontario. Canadian field-naturalist,
v. 69, p. 135-139. 1955.

Baillie, J. L.
   Recent additions to Ontario's bird list.
Ontario field biologist, no. 11, p. 1-3. 1957.
illus.

Baillie, J. L.
   Six old yet new Ontario breeding birds. Ontario
field biologist, no. 12, p. 1-7. 1958.

Barlow, J. C.
   Extralimital occurrences of the house sparrow
in northern Ontario. Ontario field biologist,
no. 20, p. 1-3. Dec. 1966.

Barlow, J. C.
   Rufous hummingbird in Ontario. Canadian field-
naturalist, v. 81, p. 148-149. 1967.

Barnston, George
   Recollections of the swans and geese of Hudson's
Bay. Ibis, v. 2, p. 253-259. 1860.

Bremner, R. M.
    Observations on the birds of the Casummit-Birch Lakes region of northwest Ontario. Canadian field-naturalist, v. 63, p. 161-165. 1949.

Brewster, William
    An undescribed form of the black duck (<u>Anas obscura</u>). Auk, v. 19, p. 183-188. 1902.

Cooch, Graham
    Spring record of Ross goose from James Bay, Ontario. Condor, v. 57, p. 191. 1955.

Currie, Campbell. <u>See</u> Hanson, H. C. and Campbell Currie

Dear, L. S.
    Bonaparte's gull breeding in Ontario. Auk, v. 56, p. 186. 1939.

East, Ben
    Waveys over the Bay. Beaver, outfit 282, p. 10-13. Sept. 1951. illus.

Forster, J. R.
    An account of the birds sent from Hudson's Bay; with observations relative to their natural history; and Latin descriptions of some of the most uncommon. Royal Society of London. Philosophical transactions, v. 62, p. 382-433. 1772.

Gagnon, Andrew. <u>See</u> Hanson, H. C. and Andrew Gagnon

Godfrey, W. E.
    The Nevada cowbird at James Bay, Ontario. Canadian field-naturalist, v. 65, p. 46. 1951.

Hanson, H. C. and R. H. Smith
    Canada geese of the Mississippi flyway; with
special reference to an Illinois flock. Bulletin
of the Illinois Natural History Survey, v. 25,
p. 67-210. 1950. illus., maps.

Hanson, H. C. and Andrew Gagnon
    The hunting and utilization of wild geese by
the Indians of the Hudson Bay lowlands of northern
Ontario. Ontario fish and wildlife review, v. 3,
no. 2, p. 2-11. Summer 1964. illus.

Hanson, H. C. and Campbell Currie
    The kill of wild geese by the natives of the
Hudson-James Bay region. Arctic, v. 10, p. 211-
229. 1957. illus.

Hanson, H. C.
    Muskeg as sharp-tailed grouse habitat. Wilson
bulletin, v. 65, p. 235-41. 1953. illus.

Hanson, H. C., Murray Rogers and E. S. Rogers
    Waterfowl of the forested portions of the
Canadian Pre-Cambrian shield and the Paleozoic
basin. Canadian field-naturalist, v. 63, p. 183-
204. 1949. illus., maps.

Hess, Quimby
    Canada geese summering in northern Ontario.
Canadian field-naturalist, v. 57, p. 46. 1943.

Hewitt, O. H.
    A local migration of the brown-headed chickadee
in James Bay. Canadian field-naturalist, v. 62,
p. 123-124. 1948.

Hewitt, O. H.
    Recent studies of blue and lesser snow goose
populations in James Bay. Transactions of the 15th
North American Wildlife Conference, p. 304-309.
1950. map.

Holmes, P. M.
    Waterfowl conservation on James Bay. RCMP quarterly, v. 16, p. 319-324. April 1951. illus.

Hope, C. E. and T. M. Shortt
    Southward migration of adult shorebirds on the west coast of James Bay, Ontario. Auk, v. 61, p. p. 572-576. 1944.

Lapworth, E. D. See Snyder, L. L. and E. D. Lapworth

Lemieux, Louis
    Taxonomie des oies blanches. Naturaliste canadien, v. 83, p. 61-65. 1956.

Lewis, H. F. and H. S. Peters
    Notes on birds of the James Bay region in the autumn of 1940. Canadian field-naturalist, v. 55, p. 111-117. 1941.

Lewis, H. F.
    Notes on September birds along Ontario's seacoast. Canadian field-naturalist, v. 53, p. 50-53. 1939.

Lewis, H. F.
    Occurrence of the European starling (Sturnus vulgaris) in the James Bay region. Auk, v. 49, p. 225. 1932.

Lewis, H. F.
    Waterfowl at James Bay. Provancher Society of Natural History of Canada. Annual report for 1938, p. 172-175.

Lewis, H. F.
    White pelican at James Bay, Canada. Auk, v. 61, p. 304-305. 1944.

Lumsden, H. G.
    Mandt's black guillemot breeding on the Hudson

Bay coast of Ontario. Canadian field-naturalist, v. 73, p. 54-55. 1959.

Lumsden, H. G.
    Ruff and white pelican at Fort Severn. Canadian field-naturalist, v. 69, p. 168. 1955.

Lumsden, H. G.
    A snow goose breeding colony in Ontario. Canadian field-naturalist, v. 71, p. 153-154.

Manning, T. H.
    Birds of the west James Bay and southern Hudson Bay coasts. Ottawa [Queen's Printer] 1952. 114 p. illus., map. (Canada. National Museum. Bulletin no. 125)

* Mickle, G. R.
    Possibilities of northern Ontario as a breeding ground for ducks. Toronto, King's Printer, 1912. 8 p.

Norris-Elye, L. T. S.
    A few bird records from the Arctic. Canadian field-naturalist, v. 46, p. 142. 1932.

Peters, H. S. See Lewis, H. F. and H. S. Peters

Rae, John
    Notes on some of the birds and mammals of the Hudson's Bay Company's territory and of the arctic coast of America. Canadian record of science, v. 3, p. 125-136. 1888.

Rogers, E. S. See Hanson, H. C., Murray Rogers and E. S. Rogers

Rogers, Murray. See Hanson, H. C., Murray Rogers and E. S. Rogers

Romig, J. G.
　　James Bay geese.　Beaver, outfit 277, p. 22-25.
　Sept. 1946.　illus.

Saunders, W. E.
　　Wild geese at Moose Factory.　Auk, v. 34, p. 334-335.　1917.

Shortt, T. M.
　　Arctic tern banded in Greenland, recovered in Ontario.　Bird-banding, v. 20, p. 50.　1949.

Shortt, T. M.　See also Hope, C. E. and T. M. Shortt

Smith, R. H.　See Hanson, H. C. and R. H. Smith

Snyder, L. L. and E. D. Lapworth
　　A comparative study of adults of two Canadian races of red-wings.　Canadian field-naturalist, v. 67, p. 143-147.　1953.　illus.

Snyder, L. L.
　　Golden eagle reported nesting in Ontario.　Auk, v. 57, p. 565-566.　1940.

Snyder, L. L.
　　A plan of Ontario subdivisions and their names for naturalists.　Canadian field-naturalist, v. 53, p. 22-24.　1939.　map.

Snyder, L. L.
　　Ross's Goose in Ontario.　Canadian field-naturalist, v. 69, p. 26-27,　1955.

Snyder, L. L.
　　A study of the sharp-tailed grouse.　Toronto, University of Toronto Press, 1935.　66 p.　illus., maps.　(University of Toronto Studies.　Biological Series, no. 40)

Stirrett, G. M.
    Field observations on geese in James Bay, with
special reference to the blue goose. Transactions
of the 19th North American Wildlife Conference,
p. 211-221. 1954.

Stirrett, G. M.
    Rough-legged hawk migration in James Bay area.
Canadian field-naturalist, v. 66, p. 87. 1952.

Sutton, G. M.
    The blue goose expedition. Cardinal, no. 3,
p. 16-18. January 1924.

Todd, W. E. C.
    Eastern races of the ruffled grouse. Auk,
v. 57, p. 390-397. 1940.

Todd, W. E. C.
    The western element in the James Bay avifauna.
Canadian field-naturalist, v. 57, p. 79-80. 1943.

SEE ALSO

Murray, Andrew
    Contributions to the natural history of the
Hudson's Bay Company's territories.
    MAMMALOGY

Preble, E. A.
    A biological investigation of the Hudson Bay
region
    MAMMALOGY

PALEONTOLOGY

Bell, Robert
    On the occurrence of mammoth and mastodon remains around Hudson Bay. Bulletin of the Geological Society of America, v. 9, p. 369-90. 1898. illus.

Bell, W. A.
    Mesozoic plants from the Mattagami series, Ontario. Canada. Geological Survey. Bulletin no. 49, p. 27-30, 58-67. 1928. illus.

Cranswick, J. S.
    The coral fauna of the Abitibi River limestone. [Toronto] 1953. 75 ℓ. illus. (University of Toronto. M. A. thesis)

Cranswick, J. S. and M. A. Fritz
    Coral fauna of the upper Abitibi River limestone. Proceedings of the Geological Association of Canada, v. 10, p. 31-81. 1958. illus.

Cranswick, J. S. See also Fritz, M. A. and J. S. Cranswick

Dowling, D. B. See Whiteaves, J. F.

Foerste, A. F.
    Devonian cephalopods from the Moose River basin. Ontario. Department of Mines. Annual report, v. 37, pt. 6, p. 70-99. 1928. illus.

Foerste, A. F. and T. E. Savage
    Ordovician and Silurian cephalopods of the Hudson Bay area. Denison University. Journal

of the scientific laboratories, v. 22, p. 1-107.
1927. illus.

Foerste, A. F.
　　Several new Silurian cephalopods and crinoids,
chiefly from Ohio and Hudson Bay. Ohio journal
of science, v. 36, p. 261-275. 1936. illus.

Fritz, M. A. and J. S. Cranswick
　　Lower and Middle Devonian of the James Bay
lowland. Proceedings of the Geological Association
of Canada, v. 6, pt. 1, p. 69-74. 1953. illus.

Fritz, M. A., R. R. H. Lemon and A. W. Norris
　　Stratigraphy and paeontology of the Williams
Island formation. Proceedings of the Geological
Association of Canada, v. 9, p. 21-27. 1957.
illus.

Fritz, M. A. and R. H. Waines
　　Stromatoporoids from the upper Abitibi River
limestone. Proceedings of the Geological Association of Canada, v. 8, p. 87-126. 1956. illus.

Fritz, M. A. See also Cranswick, J. S. and M. A.
　　Fritz

Lee, Denard
　　Some new species of corals from the Niagaran
strata of the Hudson Bay region. Transactions of
the Illinois State Academy of Science, v. 24,
p. 360-362. 1931. illus.

Lemon, R. R. H. See Fritz, M. A., R. R. H. Lemon
　　and A. W. Norris

Norris, A. W. See Fritz, M. A., R. R. H. Lemon and
　　A. W. Norris

Parks, W. A.
　　Devonian fauna of Kwataboahegan River. Ontario.

Department of Mines. Annual report, v. 13, pt. 1, p. 180-191. 1904.

Parks, W. A.
　　Notes on Silurian stromatoporoids from Hudson's Bay. Canadian field-naturalist, v. 22, p. 25-29. 1908.

Parks, W. A.
　　Paleozoic fossils from a region southwest of Hudson Bay. Transactions of the Royal Canadian Institute, v. 11, p. 1-96. 1915. illus., map.

Parks, W. A.
　　A remarkable parasite from the Devonian rocks of the Hudson Bay slope. American journal of science, v. 18, p. 135-140. 1904. illus.

Radforth, N. W.
　　Palaeobotanical evaluation of fossil wood in Onakawana lignites. Transactions of the Royal Society of Canada, ser. 3, v. 52, sect. 5, p. 41-53. illus.

Richards, H. G.
　　Recent and Pleistocene marine shells of James Bay. American midland naturalist, v. 17, p. 528-545. 1936. illus.

Savage, T. E.　See also Foerste, A. F. and T. E. Savage

Waines, R. H.　See Fritz, M. A., and R. H. Waines

Whiteaves, J. F.
　　Preliminary list of fossils from the Silurian (Upper Silurian) rocks of the Ekwan River and Sutton Mill Lakes, Keewatin, collected by D. B. Dowling in 1901, with descriptions of such species as appear to be new. Canada. Geological Survey. Annual report, n.s., v. 14, pt. F, p. 38-59.

Wilson, A. E.
   A report on fossil collections from the James Bay lowlands. Ontario. Department of Mines. Annual report, v. 61, pt. 6, p. 59-81. 1952. *In* Martison, N. W. Petroleum possibilities of the James Bay lowland area. Ontario. Department of Mines. Annual report, v. 61, pt. 6, p. 1-113.

TRANSPORTATION

Canadian Transportation
    Moosonee: trigger for a chain reaction?
Canadian transportation, v. 63, p. 40-41. Aug.
1960. illus.

Canadian Transportation
    The ONR: quiet consistent service. Canadian
transportation, v. 61, p. 25-28. July 1953.
illus.

Canadian Weekly Bulletin
    Along the Abitibi. Canada. Department of
External Affairs. Information Division. Canadian
weekly bulletin, v. 14, no. 44, p. 5. November
4, 1959.

Canadian Weekly Bulletin
    Ocean port at Moosonee. Canada. Department of
External Affairs. Information Division. Canadian
weekly bulletin, v. 14, no. 6, p. 5. February 11,
1959.

Clement, S. B.
    Construction of T. & N. O. Railway extension to
James Bay. Canadian engineer, v. 66, no. 20, p. 1-6. May 15, 1934. illus., map.

Cole, A. A.
    Ontario's route to the sea. Canadian geographical journal, v. 5, p. 130-153. 1932. illus., maps.

Dainton, Douglas
    Transportation facilities in northeastern
Ontario. Monetary times, v. 128, p. 87-89. May
1960. illus.

Ells, S. C.
    James Bay surveys; exploration trip, Cochrane to James Bay, June 9th to Sept. 12th, 1911. Ontario. Northland Transportation Commission. Annual report, v. 10, p. 91-124. 1911. illus., maps.
    Later published separately as his Report on James Bay surveys exploration: Cochrane to James Bay. June 9th to Sept. 12th, 1911. Toronto, King's Printer, 1912. 36 p. illus., maps.

Financial Post
    By rail to the frontier. Financial post, v. 59, p. 20-21. Apr. 24 suppl., 1965. illus.

Financial Post
    It's an era of change for province's railway. Financial post, v. 58, p. 59. Oct. 3, 1964.

Financial Post
    Northern Ontario trip is a frontier adventure. Financial post, v. 58, p. 31. May 9, 1964. illus.

Financial Post
    ONR adopts tricolor fares to boost passenger traffic. Financial post, v. 57, p. 19. April 27, 1963.

Financial Post
    ONR expanding communications. Financial post, v. 56, p. 42. Sept. 1, 1962.

Financial Post
    With highway network built, tourist potential goes up. Financial post, v. 59, p. 74. Oct. 2, 1965. maps.

Gilbertson, F.
    Start Moosonee survey; plan railway expansion. Financial post, v. 53, p. 1, 8. Feb. 8, 1959.

Transportation

Langford, C. J.
    Moose River and its approaches; survey of tides, currents, density and silt. Ottawa, Canadian Hydrographic Service, 1963. 94 p. illus., maps.

Monetary Times
    North Bay to Moosonee ONR trip is eye-opener. Monetary times, v. 130, p. 77. Nov. 1962.

Ontario. Northland Transportation Commission
    The end of an era; "last run" of the steam locomotive on Ontario Northland Railway, June 24th-25th, 1957. [North Bay, Ontario, 1957] 12 p. illus.

Ontario. Northland Transportation Commission
    James Bay surveys. Its Annual report, v. 10, p. 22-25. 1911.

* Storage Battery Power
    Temiskaming & Northern Ontario passenger trains operate in winter temperatures as low as -55 F; insulated, snow-tight battery compartments and positive generator drives result in successful battery operation. Storage battery power, v. 15, no. 5, p. 11-13. Dec. 1945. illus.

Sullivan, E. A. E.
    Engineer's report of exploration survey to James Bay. Ontario. Northland Transportation Commission. Annual report, v. 4, p. 54-57. 1905.

Thomson, J. G.
    Winter roads over muskeg. Canadian mining and metallurgical bulletin, v. 50, p. 159-162. 1957. Transactions of the Canadian Institute of Mining and Metallurgy, v. 60, p. 101-104. 1957.

Tyrrell, J. B.
    Arrivals and departures of ships; Moose Factory, Hudson Bay, province of Ontario. Ontario history, v. 14, p. 163-168. 1916.

Williamson, O. T. G.
    Development of Moosonee as an ocean port; a review of investigations since 1911 and of steps taken in 1958 to promote the undertaking. Ontario. Northland Transportation Commission. Annual report, 58, p. 21-46. 1958. map.

Williamson, O. T. G.
    Moosonee - a progress report; progress made during 1959 for the ultimate establishment of an ocean port and city at Moosonee. Ontario. Northland Transportation Commission. Annual report, 59, p. 19-21. 1959.

* Williamson, O. T. G.
    A new prospect for James Bay. The quarterly [Ontario Northland Railway] no. 61, p. 5, 12-13. June 1961.

Williamson, O. T. G.
    Potentialities of Moosonee... Monetary times, v. 128, p. 78, 80-81. May 1960. illus., map.

Wilson, L. A.
    Ottawa may finance 50% of Moosonee port scheme. Financial post, v. 53, p. 1. Feb. 14, 1959.

SEE ALSO

Financial Post
    Propose Moosonee seaport as new industrial centre
    ECONOMICS AND DEVELOPMENT

Financial Post
    Survey problem of dredging Moosonee deep water harbor
    ECONOMICS AND DEVELOPMENT

Transporation

Macfie, John
    Fawn River
    HISTORY

McMillan, J. G.
    Investigations at James Bay during 1912
    METEOROLOGY

Montgomery, Paul
    Ontario's newest north
    ECONOMICS AND DEVELOPMENT

Northeastern Ontario Development Association
    A report on the possible effects of a seaport
  at Moosonee on the economy of northeastern Ontario
    ECONOMICS AND DEVELOPMENT

Ontario. Department of Commerce and Development and
   others
    Report of Moosonee harbour investigation
    ECONOMICS AND DEVELOPMENT

Pain, S. A.
    The way north
    ECONOMICS AND DEVELOPMENT

Polar Record
    The use of motor tractors in northern Ontario
    ECONOMICS AND DEVELOPMENT

AUTHOR INDEX

Adam, Lucien. 87
Adams, H. P. 49
Adams, J. I. 59
Adams, J. Q. 55
Allington, K. R. 93
Anderson, David. 46
Anderson, J. W. 26, 46
Arctic Circular. 26, 92
Armstrong, H. S. 59
Arthur, E. R. 80
Auer, Vaino. 3
Baillie, J. L. 98
Bajkov, Alexander. 83
Baker, F. C. 85
Baker, M. B. 46, 59
Baldwin, W. K. W. 3
Baldwin, W. W. 26
Balicki, Asen. 26
Barlow, J. C. 98
Barnell, J. D. 46
Barnston, George. 90, 98
Bateman, J. D. 59
Batty, Beatrice (Stebbing). 46
Bean, T. H. 83
Beaulieu, Vincent. 46
Bedell, G. H. D. 45
Bell, J. M. 60
Bell, Robert. 12, 24, 26, 47, 60, 105
Bell, W. A. 105
Belleau, Henri. 80
Bennett, G. 60
Bentley, J. M. 47
Beveridge, Thomas. 80
Birket-Smith, Kaj. 26
Blais, J. R. 44, 45
Bloomfield, Leonard. 87
Blue, Archibald. 47
Boissonneau, A. N. 20
Boivin, Bernard. 3
Bolton, L. L. 47
Boon, T. C. B. 80
Borron, E. B. 3, 47, 48
Boucher, G. P. 56
Boville, B. W. 93
Bradley, G. A. 24
Bremner, R. M. 99
Brewster, William. 99
Brown, D. D. 60
Bruce, E. L. 60, 61
Bruemmer, Fred. 48
Buckman, Eduard. 48
Burwash, E. M. 48, 61
Cahn, A. R. 85
Cameron, Duncan. 27
Camsell, Charles. 48
Canada. Dept. of Citizenship and Immigration. Indian affairs branch. 27
Canada. Dept. of Indian Affairs. 27
Canada. Dept. of Indian Affairs and Northern Development. 27
Canada. Geological Survey. 61

Canada. Ontario-Manitoba Boundary Commission, 1954. 8
Canada. Parliament. House of Commons. Select Committee on boundaries between Ontario and unorganized territories. 8
Canadian Transportation. 109
Canadian Weekly Bulletin. 109
Carlson, H. D. 61
Carrière, Gaston. 80
Caron, Ivanhoe. 53
Carruthers, Janet. 55
Chamberlain, A. F. 87
Chance, N. A. 27
Chapman, Howard. 80
Chapman, L. J. 93
Charlewood, G. H. 62
Charlton, J. L. 48
Charlton, W. A. 48
Chisholm, E. O. 62
Chisholm, Paul. 12
Churcher, C. S. 90
Clarkson, S. W. 12
Clement, S. B. 109
Coates, D. F. 55
Cole, A. A. 48, 109
Coleman, A. P. 62
Collins, W. H. 62, 63
Cooch, Graham. 99
Cooke, H. C. 63
Coombs, D. B. 55
Cooper, J. M. 27, 28, 29
Cotter, J. L. 48
Cranswick, J. S. 105, 106

Cringan, A. T. 13
Crooks, G. E. 12
Cross, J. G. 63
Crossman, E. J. 83
Crozier, A. R. 63, 65
Curran, C. H. 24
Curran, G. B. 13
Curran, W. T. 49
Currie, Campbell. 100
Dainton, Douglas. 109
Davey, E. R. 63
Dean, W. G. 55
Dear, L. S. 99
Derry, D. R. 64
de Vos, Anton. 13
Dewdney, Selwyn. 1
Douglas, G. V. 64
Douglass, D. P. 13
Dowling, D. B. 49, 64, 107
Downing, S. C. 90
Duffell, S. 13
Duman, Maximilian. 4
Dunning, R. W. 29
Dutilly, A. A. 4
Dyer, W. S. 64, 65
Dymond, J. R. 83, 90
East, Ben. 99
Eastman, C. A. 30
Edwards, B. G. 66
Ellis, C. D. 30, 87, 88
Ells, S. C. 110
Elton, C. S. 90
Enright, C. T. 13
Erentz, C. 17
Evans, E. L. 66
Faries, R. 88
Fernow, B. E. 49
Field, F. W. 13
Financial Post. 8, 14, 15, 110

Author Index

Fisher, M. W. 30
Flannery, Regina. 30
Flint, R. F. 66
Foerste, A. F. 105, 106
Foerste, J. W. 31
Forster, J. R. 31, 90, 99
Fraser, C. G. 49
Fritz, M. A. 105, 106
Furse, G. D. 66
Gagnon, Andrew. 100
Gardiner, L. M. 24
Gardner, Gerard. 55
Gates, R. R. 31
George, P. T. 60
Gibbon, M. E. 31, 80
Gibson, T. W. 49
Gilbert, Geoffrey. 66
Gilbertson, F. 110
Gilchrist, Lachlan. 66
Gilmore, R. E. 67
Godfrey, W. E. 99
Godsell, P. H. 31
Godson, W. L. 93
Goodrich, Calvin. 85
Goodwin, A. M. 67
Gosselin, A. 56
Gould, E. C. 15
Grant, Peter. 32
Great Britain. Privy Council. 8
Green, J. A. 49
Greig, J. W. 67
Gussow, W. C. 67
Haddow, W. R. 44
Hallowell, A. I. 32, 33, 34, 35
Hanson, H. C. 100
Harding, W. D. 67
Hare, F. K. 93

Harrington, Lyn. 49
Harrington, Richard. 49, 50
Harvey, Paul. 50
Hatfield, S. S. 15
Hawley, J. E. 61, 68
Henderson, Archibald. 15
Hess, Quimby. 100
Hewitt, O. H. 100
Hill, G. A. 20
Hills, G. A. 16
Hincks, Francis. 8
Hoffman, Hans. 36
Holman, R. H. C. 13
Holmes, E. M. 36
Holmes, P. M. 101
Honigmann, J. J. 36, 37
Hope, C. E. 100
Hopkins, P. E. 68
Horden, J. A. 88
Horwood, H. C. 68
Howard, S. H. 37
Hudec, P. P. 78
Hughes, O. L. 69, 76
Hunter, James. 88
Hurst, M. E. 69
Hustich, Ilmari. 4, 56
Ireton, H. J. C. 94
Jamieson, N. M. 50
Jenkins, D. W. 24
Jenkins, W. H. 37
Jenness, Diamond. 37
Jessup, Britt. 16
Johnson, A. M. 50
Johnson, C. W. 24
Johnson, Frederick. 38
Johnson, J. P. 69
Johnson, J. T. H. 53
Johnston, R. N. 45
Kane, H. B. 50
Keele, Joseph. 69, 70

Kenoyer, L. A.   4
Kenyon, W. A.   2
Kerr, H. L.   50
Kidd, K. E.   1
Kindle, E. M.   56, 70
Kirkconnell, T. W.   4
Knapton, G.   16
Knight, H. H.   24
Knight, K. L.   25
Komhyr, W. D.   93, 94
Kurata, T. B.   85
Laird, H. C.   70
Langelier, J. C.   56
Langford, C. J.   111
Langford, F. F.   70
Lapworth, E. D.   103
La Rocque, A.   71, 85
Laviolette, Gontran.   38
Lee, Denard.   106
Lee, H. A.   71
Lee, T. E.   1
Leechman, Douglas.   38, 41
Leitch, Adelaide.   50
Leith, C. K.   71
Lemieux, Louis.   101
Lemon, R. R. H.   106
Lendrum, Frank.   88
Lepage, Ernest.   4, 5
Lewis, H. F.   101
Liebow, Elliott.   38
Lindsey, Charles.   9
Logan, R. A.   88, 89
Long Lance, Buffalo Child.   38
Low, A. P.   71
Lower, A. R. M.   50, 83
Luke, L. W.   16
Lumsden, H. G.   101, 102

Lyon-Fellows, Evelyn.   80
McAdam, Catherine.   16
Macaulay, R. W.   16
McDermott, G. L.   56
Macfie, John.   38, 50, 81
McGugan, B. M.   45
McInnes, William.   51, 71
Mackay, Hugh.   51
Mackenzie, G. S.   64
MacLaren, A. S.   13
MacLean, D. W.   45
McLearn, F. H.   71
McLennan, J. C.   94
MacMahon, Hugh.   9
McMillan, J. G.   94
MacNeish, R. S.   2
Macoun, J. M.   5
Maher, W. R.   94
Malcolm, Wyatt.   72
Manning, T. H.   56, 102
Marsh, W. H. C.   16, 17
Martison, N. W.   72
Marwick, Alice.   81
Massey, Hart.   80
Mathews, R. K.   81
Mawdsey-Jones, R. H.   17
Meen, V. B.   72
Michelson, Truman.   39, 89
Mickle, G. R.   5, 102
Millar, John.   92
Millar, J. B.   45
Miller, W. G.   51
Mills, David.   9
Mills, Edwin.   51
Moir, D. R.   6, 56
Monetary Times.   17, 18, 111
Montgomery, Paul.   18
Montgomery, R. J.   72
Moore, E. S.   72
Moorhouse, W. W.   73

Morris, Alexander. 39
Morris, J. L. 39
Morris, W. J. 39
Munday, Albert. 90
Natural Resources, Canada. 9, 19, 57
Ness, M. E. 39
Nevins, J. B. 51
Newnham, J. A. 53
Nichols, D. A. 57
Nickle, W. M. 19
Nipissing & James Bay Railway. 52
Norris, A. W. 106
Norris-Elye, L. T. S. 102
Northeastern Ontario Development Association. 19
Notman, Howard. 25
Ogilvie, N. J. 94
Ogilvie, William. 57
Omand, D. M. 39
Ontario. 9, 10
Ontario. Attorney-General's Department. 10
Ontario. Attorney-General's Department, appellant vs. Manitoba. Attorney-General's Department, respondent. 10
Ontario. Commission on Kapuskasing Colony. 19
Ontario. Department of Commerce and Development. 19
Ontario. Department of Economics. Economic Survey. 19, 20
Ontario. Department of Economics and Development. Applied Economics Branch. 20
Ontario. Department of Lands and Forests. 20
Ontario. Department of Lands and Forests. Forestry Branch. 45
Ontario. Department of Mines. 73
Ontario. Legislative Assembly. 10
Ontario. Northland Transportation Commission. 111
Ontario. Provincial Secretary's Department. 10
Ontario Housing. 39
Ontario Mining Association. 52
Ontario Research Foundation. 73
Orchard, W. C. 39
Orr, R. B. 40
O'Sullivan, Owen. 52
Pain, S. A. 81
Paradis, C. A. M. 52
Parks, W. A. 52, 73, 106, 107
Paul-Emile (Soeur Louise Mary Guay) 81
Persson, Herman. 6
Peters, Austin. 53
Peters, H. S. 101
Peters, F. H. 11
Pettijohn, F. J. 73
Phillips, Alexander. 20
Polar Record. 20
Porsild, A. E. 6
Potter, David. 6, 74
Preble, E. A. 91

Author Index

Prest, V. K. 74
Proulx, J. B. 53
Radforth, N. W. 107
Rae, John. 40, 102
Ramsay, George. 92
Ramsay, T. K. 11
Randall, Peter. 53
Reed, E. B. 85
Renison, R. J. 53
Rich, E. E. 82
Richards, H. G. 57, 86, 107
Riddiough, Norman. 40
Ridley, Frank. 2, 92
Riotte, J. C. E. 25
Rittenhouse, Gordon. 75
Roads and Engineering Construction. 20
Roberts, Lloyd. 53
Robertson, E. C. 92
Rogers, E. S. 20, 40, 41, 100
Rogers, J. H. 89
Rogers, Murray. 100
Rogers, W. R. 75
Roliff, W. A. 75
Romig, J. H. 103
Rorke, L. V. 11
Ryder, R. A. 83
Saidon, Emile. 82
Saindon, J. E. 41, 89
Satterly, Jack. 75, 76
Saunders, W. E. 103
Savage, T. E. 76, 105
Scott, Lloyd. 41
Scott, W. B. 83
Sharpe, J. F. 45
Shearwood, M. H. 53
Shortt, T. M. 100, 103
Skinner, Alanson. 2, 41
Sjörs, H. M. 6
Smith, R. H. 100
Smith, R. M. 21
Snyder, L. L. 103
Société de Geographie de Québec. 53
Speight, T. B. 21
Spieth, H. T. 25
Stewart, James. 42
Stirrett, G. M. 104
Storage Battery Power. 111
Strath, R. 42
Sturrock, R. F. 93
Sullivan, E. A. E. 111
Sutton, G. M. 104
Swindlehurst, F. 42
Taylor, A. W. 80
Taylor, S. A. 42
Teicher, M. I. 42
Terasmae, Jaan. 76
Thomson, J. E. 76, 77
Thomson, J. G. 111
Thomson, R. B. 5
Thomson, Robert. 77
Thorman, G. E. 57
Tisdall, F. F. 92
Todd, W. E. C. 104
Treadwell, William. 21
Tremblay, Maurice. 21
Troyes, Pierre. 53
Trudeau, John. 27, 38, 42
Tyrrell, J. B. 77, 89, 111
Umfreville, Edward. 54
Van Tuyl, F. M. 76
Vivian, R. P. 92
Vollmer, Margaret. 82
Waines, R. H. 106
Walker, E. M. 25
Warren, W. W. 42
Watkins, E. A. 88, 89
Watson, R. J. 72
Webster, A. R. 77

www.ingramcontent.com/pod-product-compliance
Lightning Source LLC
Chambersburg PA
CBHW051352070526
44584CB00025B/3737